DOING YOUR LITERATURE REVIEW

POCKET STUDY SKILLS

Series Editor: **Kate Williams**,
Oxford Brookes University, UK
Illustrations by Sallie Godwin

For the time-pushed student, the *Pocket Study Skills* pack a lot of advice into a little book. Each guide focuses on a single crucial aspect of study giving you step-by-step guidance, handy tips and clear advice on how to approach the important areas which will continually be at the core of your studies.

Published

14 Days to Exam Success (2nd edn)
Analyzing a Case Study
Blogs, Wikis, Podcasts and More
Brilliant Writing Tips for Students (2nd edn)
Completing Your PhD
Doing Research (2nd edn)
Doing Your Literature Review
Getting Critical (3rd edn)
How to Analyze Data
Managing Stress
Planning Your Dissertation (3rd edn)
Planning Your Essay (4th edn)
Planning Your PhD
Posters and Presentations

Reading and Making Notes (3rd edn)
Referencing and Understanding Plagiarism (2nd edn)
Reflective Writing (2nd edn)
Report Writing (2nd edn)
Science Study Skills
Studying with Dyslexia (3rd edn)
Success in Groupwork (2nd edn)
Successful Applications
Time Management
Using Feedback to Boost Your Grades
Where's Your Evidence?
Writing for University (3rd edn)

# POCKET STUDY SKILLS

Vanessa van der Ham and Josta Heyligers

DOING YOUR LITERATURE REVIEW

BLOOMSBURY ACADEMIC
LONDON • NEW YORK • OXFORD • NEW DELHI • SYDNEY

BLOOMSBURY ACADEMIC
Bloomsbury Publishing Plc, 50 Bedford Square, London, WC1B 3DP, UK
Bloomsbury Publishing Inc, 1359 Broadway, New York, NY 10018, USA
Bloomsbury Publishing Ireland, 29 Earlsfort Terrace, Dublin 2, D02 AY28, Ireland

BLOOMSBURY, BLOOMSBURY ACADEMIC and the Diana logo are trademarks of Bloomsbury Publishing Plc

First published in Great Britain 2026

Copyright © Vanessa van der Ham and Josta Heyligers, 2026

Vanessa van der Ham and Josta Heyligers have asserted their right under the Copyright, Designs and Patents Act, 1988, to be identified as Authors of this work.

Cover design: Jade Barnett

All rights reserved. No part of this publication may be: i) reproduced or transmitted in any form, electronic or mechanical, including photocopying, recording or by means of any information storage or retrieval system without prior permission in writing from the publishers; or ii) used or reproduced in any way for the training, development or operation of artificial intelligence (AI) technologies, including generative AI technologies. The rights holders expressly reserve this publication from the text and data mining exception as per Article 4(3) of the Digital Single Market Directive (EU) 2019/790.

Bloomsbury Publishing Plc does not have any control over, or responsibility for, any third-party websites referred to or in this book. All internet addresses given in this book were correct at the time of going to press. The author and publisher regret any inconvenience caused if addresses have changed or sites have ceased to exist, but can accept no responsibility for any such changes.

A catalogue record for this book is available from the British Library.

Library of Congress Cataloging-in-Publication Data

ISBN: PB: 978-1-3504-5661-7
        ePDF: 978-1-3504-5660-0
        eBook: 978-1-3504-5662-4

Series: Pocket Study Skills

Typeset by Integra Software Services Pvt. Ltd.
Printed and bound in India

For product safety related questions contact productsafety@bloomsbury.com.

To find out more about our authors and books visit www.bloomsbury.com and sign up for our newsletters.

Contents

Acknowledgements vi
Introduction vii
What is the literature on a topic? ix
Steps in the literature review process xiii

Part 1 Getting started 1

1 Clarify your task and audience expectations 1
2 Choose your topic 22
3 Focus your topic into an answerable question 25

Part 2 Finding and selecting your sources 35

4 Design your search strategy 36
5 Search the library databases 42
6 Evaluate and select your sources 47

Part 3 Reading and making notes 62

7 Engage with your sources 64

Part 4 Planning your literature review 73

8 Identify themes and subthemes 75
9 Plan the structure of your review 80

Part 5 Writing your literature review 87

10 Drafting your literature review 87
11 Editing your literature review 124

References 128
Index 130

Acknowledgements

We'd like to thank the many people who've contributed to this guide. A special thanks to Andrew Lenton for allowing us to use adapted extracts from his thesis and for his feedback on our ideas. Thanks also to all the students whose questions and comments over the years have guided our practice and informed our advice in the guide. A big thanks to our AUT colleagues working in information literacy who helped us with advice on finding and selecting sources: Dr Steph Clout, Camilo Amaya Lara, and Elwyn Sheehan. Our thanks also to colleagues Dr Andre Breedt and Craig Wattam for their advice on the use of Gen AI in assessments, and Dr Jenny Mendieta for her feedback on our ideas.

Thanks also to Helen Caunce, Kate Williams and Molly Luck from Bloomsbury for their guidance, and to Sallie Godwin for her illustrations.

Finally, a huge thanks to our partners Mark van der Ham and Richard Barber for their support throughout the writing process.

Introduction

A literature review is an overview of what researchers and experts have published on a topic. Doing your literature review involves finding, evaluating and bringing together information from a range of published sources to present an argument about:

- what is currently known about your topic
- the quality and extent of this knowledge.

You might be doing a literature review to:

> Make informed decisions on current issues or problems

> Situate your own research project in the existing knowledge on your topic

How will my interviews with this group of parents contribute to our current understanding of why children quit sport at school?

> Justify the design of a new product or design

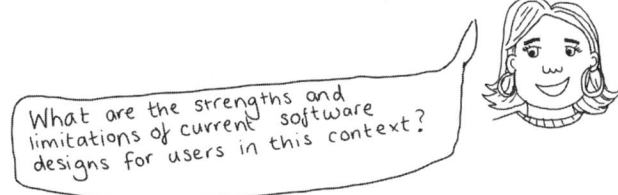

What are the strengths and limitations of current software designs for users in this context?

Your literature review demonstrates to the reader that you have the skills to:
- identify an answerable question on a problem or issue
- locate the best evidence available on the topic
- use this evidence to provide a persuasive argument on the problem or issue
- evaluate the evidence.

You are presenting **your** perspective on the existing literature:

A **summary** of relevant information on your topic

synthesised (brought together) into arguments on themes or issues you identify in the literature

and **evaluated** in terms of its quality and contribution to knowledge on your topic.

What is the literature on a topic?

A useful way of thinking about the literature is that it is made up of ongoing **conversations** between researchers on a topic. Burke (1941) compared research to 'entering a room full of voices on the topic'. Each researcher or group of researchers entering the room contributes to existing knowledge, building on what has already been said about the topic.

They're talking about their own research and how it fits in with other research on the topic:
- their findings from studies on the topic
- their reviews of studies on the topic
- the theories and concepts they're using, refining or developing in their research.

Introduction

You'll find these conversations in journal articles, academic books and other **sources** in your library databases. Each source makes a contribution or several contributions to understanding on the topic.

In your literature review, you're synthesising and evaluating the contribution of your selected sources to provide the reader with a critical overview of current knowledge on your topic:

Literature on your topic		**You're answering questions about:**
Theories Related concepts Research findings Reviews of research Arguments Legislation Professional codes Protocols Standards	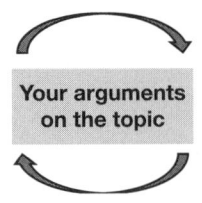 **Your arguments on the topic**	● Who's talking and who are the dominant voices in the conversation? ● What are the issues/concerns they are raising on the topic? ● Where do they agree and disagree on these issues? ● What have they contributed to the conversation? ● What are the gaps these voices haven't addressed yet? Why are these gaps important?

Depending on the purpose and requirements of your literature review and your level of study, you may be referring to a limited number of sources on your topic, or a large number for a more comprehensive review.

This book provides annotated samples of writing to show you what synthesis and evaluation of sources on a topic might look like, and suggests useful techniques and tools, including the use of generative artificial intelligence (gen AI), to help you get there.

Steps in the literature review process

Doing Your Literature Review takes you through the important steps in your literature review journey, as shown in this figure.

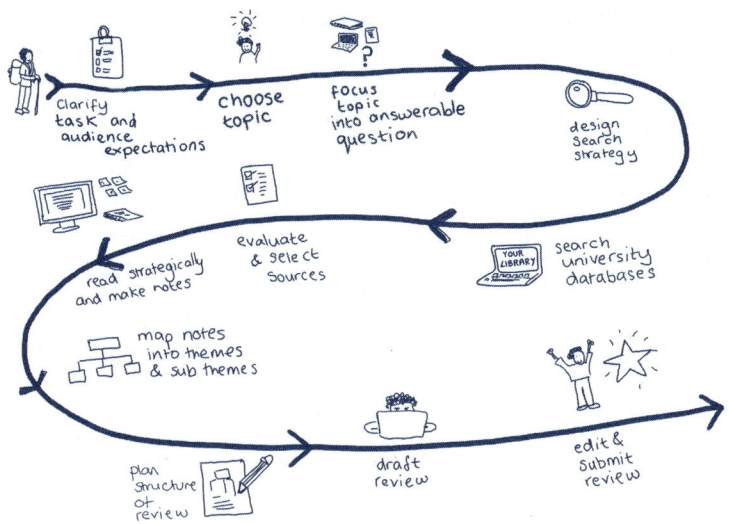

You will, of course, be going back and forth between these steps as you write your review, and we help you check your progress through these steps. Gen AI can be a useful tool as you work on your literature review but it needs to be used in ways that don't undermine the academic integrity of your work. These are a few checkpoints.

> **Are you allowed to use gen AI in your assignments?**
> Check for related policy on your university's website, in course guides and in assignment briefs.
>
> **Which tools can you use?**
> Check whether your university recommends the use of a specific tool or tools. They might also make these tools freely available through your student account. If they do, make sure you sign in and use the tool through your university account. This will take you to a safe environment where your question and gen AI answer will not be shared with others.
>
> **How can you use the tools for doing your literature review?**
> Check for specific guidelines in assignment briefs and ask your lecturer if you're not sure. As a general rule, if you are allowed to use gen AI tools for your literature review:

You can use them to help you to prepare for writing your literature review ✓	You can't use them to write your literature review for you ✗

We offer suggestions on using AI tools to help you get started on your literature review, find sources on your topic, engage with the sources, and plan your literature review. Our advice will come with cautions, particularly in terms of:
- copyright issues with uploading information to AI tools
- evaluating any information generated by AI
- acknowledging use of any AI generated content.

Part 1 Getting started is about clarifying what you need to do in your review, and how you can narrow your topic into an answerable question that fits your task and purpose.

Part 2 Finding and selecting your sources focuses on using key search words and library databases, and selecting sources that meet the requirements of your task.

Part 3 Reading strategically and making notes provides techniques and tools for reading your sources effectively and making notes relevant to your topic and task.

Part 4 Planning the review looks at strategies and tools for organising information into themes/issues on the topic and creating an outline of the review.

Part 5 Writing and editing your review focuses on synthesising and critiquing the literature in sentences and paragraphs, using your own voice to guide the reader through your arguments; writing introductions and conclusions; and tools and techniques for editing.

PART 1: GETTING STARTED

1. Clarify your task and audience expectations

Although it's tempting to rush off to the library to find sources on your topic, it's worth taking a while to make sure you're clear about what you are being asked to do.

You're bringing together the key voices on your topic to achieve a specific purpose in your literature review, a bit like the conductor of a choir. Before you choose and assemble those voices, it's important to know what you're setting out to achieve with them, and the expectations of your audience.

Literature reviews are generally structured a bit like essays in terms of their main parts:

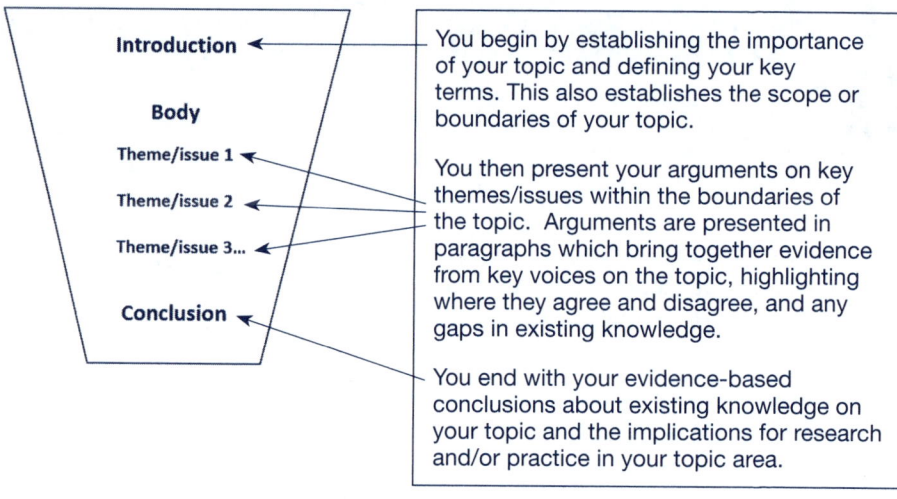

Introduction — You begin by establishing the importance of your topic and defining your key terms. This also establishes the scope or boundaries of your topic.

Body (Theme/issue 1, Theme/issue 2, Theme/issue 3...) — You then present your arguments on key themes/issues within the boundaries of the topic. Arguments are presented in paragraphs which bring together evidence from key voices on the topic, highlighting where they agree and disagree, and any gaps in existing knowledge.

Conclusion — You end with your evidence-based conclusions about existing knowledge on your topic and the implications for research and/or practice in your topic area.

What goes into these parts, how long they are, and how they are written will depend on:
- the specific purpose of your literature review task
- the requirements for achieving this purpose.

Here, we'll use examples to illustrate the purpose of the literature review in three different types of literature review tasks common in university study. We'll use the examples to illustrate advice on getting there throughout the book.

Literature reviews as part of a larger project

Many literature review tasks at university are aimed at establishing a foundation of knowledge that informs or underpins a larger project. The purpose is often to justify your recommendations or choices in the project by providing evidence from the literature; for example:
- Why your approach to a problem, case or situation is appropriate
- Why your design or system is needed for a target market
- Why your own research project is needed to fill a gap in understanding on your topic.

Example 1: A literature review leading to guidelines

Emma's larger project is to create a blog providing guidelines for parents on encouraging motivation for maths learning. The specific purpose of Emma's review is to provide a solid foundation of evidence that addresses the complexities of the topic and supports the guidelines.

Her assignment brief explains the purpose of the literature review:

> Critically review the literature on the issue to justify your recommendations.

The question Emma answers in her literature review is:

How can parents build their children's intrinsic motivation for mathematics through home-based involvement in their learning?

Her readers will expect her to answer related questions in her review in an Introduction-Body-Conclusion format:

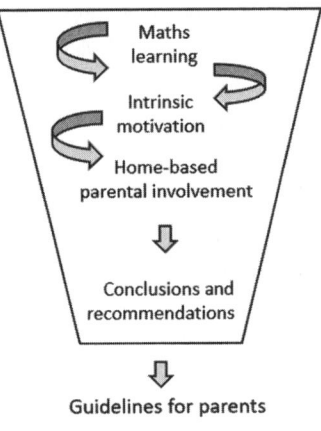

Introduction: What is intrinsic motivation, and **why** is it an issue in children's maths learning? **Why** do we need to know about the involvement of parents in the home?

Body with headings indicating theme/issues identified in the literature and paragraphs presenting arguments:
- What does the evidence say about *strategies* for parents to motivate children in this context? **How** do these practices work and **why**?
- What are the potential *barriers/challenges* for parents? **Why? How** can these be addressed?

Conclusions and recommendations about practices in parental involvement, justified by evidence presented in body.

 Explanations of **why** and **how** are crucial in critical analysis of the literature.

Clarify your task and audience expectations

Example 2: A literature review leading to own research

If you're doing a research project, the main purpose of your literature review is to convince the reader that there's a gap in existing knowledge and more research needs to be done. The gap creates a research space that your study will fill and helps justify your research aims and questions.

Your guidelines might describe this function of your literature review as a:

> Synthesis and critical evaluation of existing knowledge to establish a need for further research.

Andrew's research aimed to contribute to existing knowledge on the transition to retirement for elite athletes (see Lenton, 2016, in References). In his interviews with elite athletes in New Zealand, he aimed to find out how they transitioned into retirement from elite sport, and whether currently available interventions helped them to adjust to retirement.

His literature review needs to persuade the reader that understanding these issues is important, and that answers are not currently available in the literature – that there's a gap for his research.

He starts with the big picture of his research, then increasingly narrows his focus through what is already known on his topic, to the gap for his study:

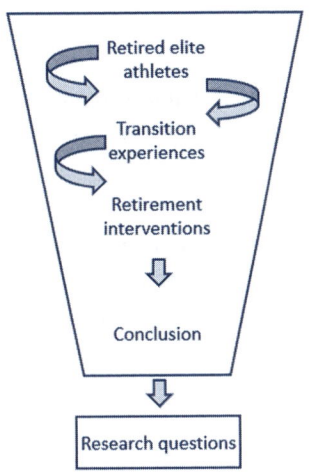

Chapter 1 Introduction establishes the importance of gaining insight into elite athletes' experiences of the transition to retirement and interventions in New Zealand – the boundaries of his topic.

Chapter 2 Literature review situates his study in existing research within these boundaries. He provides an evaluation and synthesis of:
- Theories and models of **athlete retirement** to justify the theoretical framework used in his study.
- Studies related to stages in his chosen framework, finishing with **transitions and interventions** (the focus of his own research) and leading down to the lack of New Zealand-based evidence in these areas of knowledge (the gap for his study).

Conclusion summarises the current state of knowledge on his topic and explains what his own research will contribute.

Clarify your task and audience expectations

Stand-alone literature reviews

Literature reviews can also be stand-alone tasks, where the literature review is the whole assignment.

Example 3: Critical review of the literature

The purpose of these reviews is to evaluate and synthesise existing research on a specific topic to reach a conclusion(s) about the current state of knowledge on the topic.

Generally, readers will expect:
- critical evaluation of individual studies – their strengths and limitations in terms of the quality of their research and its contribution to knowledge on the topic
- synthesis of individual findings to identify areas of agreement and disagreement on the topic
- identification of gaps or inconsistencies in findings to suggest the need for further research on the topic.

At paper level, critical reviews often focus on topics related to practice. For her critical review in a community counselling paper, Anisha has chosen the topic of PTSD among refugees. The question she answers in her critical review is:

What are the risk factors and most effective interventions for PTSD in resettled women refugees?

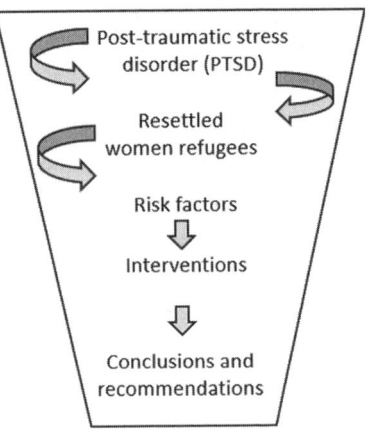

Introduction establishing significance and boundaries of topic: What is PTSD and why is it important that we investigate risk factors and interventions for this group?

Body divided into themes and subthemes presenting arguments supported by evidence from sources:
- What are the risk factors for PTSD among this group? Why? What is the extent of current understanding of these factors?
- What are the current interventions for PTSD? How do they work? What are the strengths and limitations for this group? Why?

Conclusion presenting answer to question: What can be concluded about best practice for identifying PTSD in this group and providing interventions?
Recommendations about practice and further research

Literature reviews requiring systematic methods

Increasingly, literature reviews in the areas of health and social care require students to demonstrate that they have applied a systematic approach to searching for and selecting literature to answer a question on their topic. These are generally called 'systematic reviews' of the literature.

The purpose is similar to a critical review in that you're bringing together and evaluating the evidence in the literature to find an answer to a problem or issue, often related to practice. The big difference lies in the method you use to obtain your answer from the literature.

In the health sciences, questions are commonly very specific and often centre around whether a **treatment** or **intervention** can achieve a **specific outcome** in a specific **patient or population** group.

Example 4: Review using systematic methods

For his undergraduate assignment in a healthcare paper, Karl wants to find out:

> *What is the evidence on the use of dance therapy for improving mobility in post-stroke patients?*

Approaching the review 'systematically' means that you use a predetermined and rigorous search and selection method to compile a set of existing research to address your question. This is the methodology for your review, and you will be expected to include a detailed description in your assignment so that your methodology is transparent for the reader.

For his search process, Karl needs to decide which **eligibility criteria** to apply in including and excluding sources in his review. Common criteria include databases to select, search terms to use, type of publication, method used, date published, location (place/setting) of research, and language.

Requirements for your search and selection method will vary depending on your audience and level of study, so look through assignment briefs for specific guidelines.

Reviews using systematic techniques are generally structured like a research report with Introduction - Method(ology) - Results - Discussion/Conclusion:

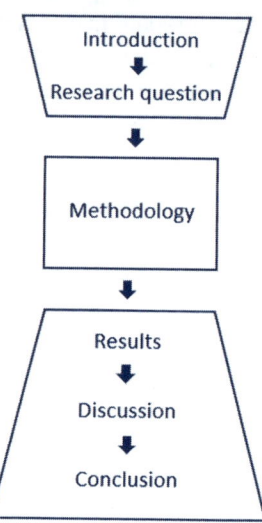

Brief introduction establishing importance of your topic and the boundaries for your review. What is the specific **question** (or questions) you're aiming to answer by bringing the literature together?

Methodology explaining **how** you brought the literature together to answer your question. Which databases did you search? What were your search terms? What were your inclusion and exclusion criteria for selecting sources to answer your question? How many sources did you find? How did you assess their quality? How many fitted your criteria?

Results and **discussion** presenting, analysing and evaluating the evidence from the literature. What were the findings of individual studies on your topic? What was the quality and extent of their contribution to understanding? How do their findings compare? What conclusions can be drawn from the studies you've included?

Conclusion presenting your answer to the question and the implications for related research and practice on your topic

It's becoming more and more common for literature review assignments and dissertations to include a description of search strategies used (key words, databases searched) and selection processes applied.

It's helpful to see a sample of the specific type of review you're doing before you choose your topic, so you can get an idea of your endpoint before you start. A few places you can check:

Course materials: Tutors sometimes provide sample assignments. They often put these with assignment guidelines and marking rubrics in the course materials.

Library websites: These sometimes offer sample assignments or extracts from assignments with useful comments in the margins. Some of these are specific to particular disciplines.

If you're doing a literature review for a research project, your library staff can show you how to search for dissertations and theses in your subject area.

Journal articles in library databases: Research articles (studies) include a literature review at the start of the article (see p. 53). You'll also find critical reviews of research and systematic reviews.

Bear in mind that the literature reviews you see in journal articles might not fit the requirements of your review. For example, systematic reviews published in journal articles are often required to have an extremely detailed methodology section and an extensive reference list to provide a comprehensive cover of the available literature on the topic.

It's easy to be intimidated by these articles, but unless you're doing a PhD, it's unlikely that anyone will expect you to produce anything this comprehensive. Your task will have specific requirements to suit your level of study and the time you have to complete the task.

How can gen AI help me?

You can prompt a gen AI tool to help you understand the structure of the type of literature review you're doing. Prompts are instructions or questions you use to tell the tool what you want it to do. The more specific you make your prompt, the more detailed the response will be.

> *I'm a student writing a review of the literature. Please suggest a structure for writing this assignment.*

You can be more specific by providing context and task descriptions:

> *I'm a **third-year** student **in the health sciences** writing **a critical** review of the literature on **PTSD among women refugees**. Please suggest a structure for **a 2,500-word** assignment **of approximately 12 paragraphs**.*

There are several gen AI prompt banks available online. Make sure you search for one providing prompts for use in the academic context.

The University of Sheffield's Gen AI academic prompt bank lists prompts for different purposes and explains issues to consider in using the information provided:
www.sheffield.ac.uk/study-skills/digital/generative-ai/prompt-bank#how-to-use-the-prompt-bank

Are there specific requirements for the literature?

If you have an assignment brief, check for instructions on:
- the type of sources you should include
- how current they need to be in terms of publication date
- how many sources you need to include.

A clear understanding of these expectations at the start of your journey is crucial because you're going to have to make sure there is enough of the required literature out there for your chosen topic.

Sources are often categorised as primary and secondary sources. The difference can be explained like this:

Primary sources	Secondary sources
'Information collected and written up by the organisation or person who carried out the work at first hand' (Williams and Reid, 2023).	Sources 'written by someone who has read the primary source(s) and summarised or described it in some way' (Williams and Reid, 2023).
For example, a journal article written by researchers who collected data from an experiment, surveys or interviews, analysed the data and reached conclusions.	For example, a review article written by researchers to present an overview of studies on a topic.

If you want to use a study cited in a secondary source, it's good practice to find the original study if possible and use that. If the study is no longer available, it is generally acceptable to use the secondary source.

For some topics, you need to consider the level of evidence required in the assignment.

Levels of evidence

'Levels of evidence' refer to a study's research design. In some areas of study, such as the sciences and applied sciences, **quantitative research**, especially experimental studies and systematic reviews of these studies, is considered to produce the most reliable findings and conclusions.

For this reason, quantitative research is placed at the top level of evidence to be used in making decisions and recommendations. **Qualitative studies** and reviews of these studies, as well as **expert opinions**, are placed lower down. The levels of evidence are shown in the figure.

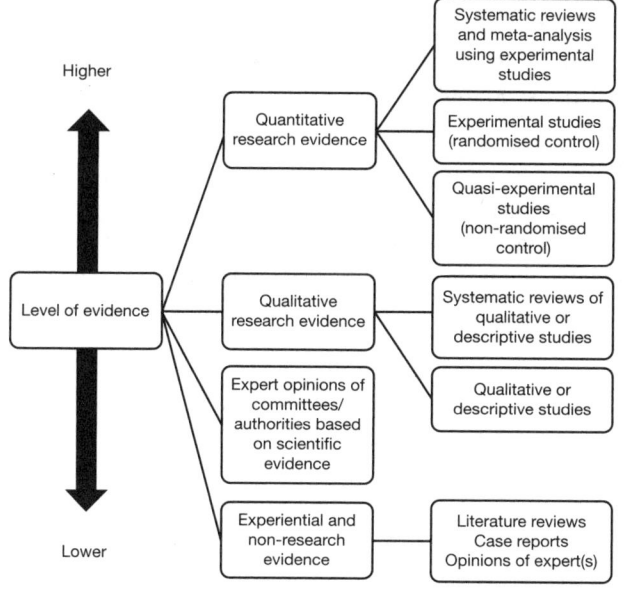

Some literature reviews require you to include only evidence at the highest levels. Many others require you to also include qualitative studies to provide deeper understanding and insights on the topic or issue.

Source: Adapted from Melnyk and Fineout-Overholt (2023) and Dang et al. (2021)

For his review of dance therapy for post-stroke patients, Karl was required to include peer-reviewed primary research, both quantitative and qualitative studies.

Article subtitles often indicate the type of research conducted. These are two of Karl's references.

Bruyneel et al. (2023) Dance after stroke improves motor recovery in the subacute phase: A randomized controlled trial. *Heliyon*, 9(11). https://doi.org/10.1016/j.heliyon.2023.e22275	Randomised controlled trials (RCTs) use experimental research to measure the effectiveness of an intervention or treatment. This is quantitative research.
Beaudry, L. et al. (2019) Adapted dance used in subacute rehabilitation post-stroke: Impacts perceived by patients, relatives and rehabilitation specialists. *Disability and Rehabilitation*, 42(155): 1–10.	The words 'perceived by' suggest qualitative research – an exploration of people's experiences of a therapy (**how** they felt about it and **why** they felt that way). This kind of research can contribute to understanding the acceptability and effectiveness of interventions for people in their specific contexts (World Health Organization, 2018).

Although qualitative research cannot stand on its own in terms of determining the efficacy of interventions, it's increasingly recognised in healthcare as an important source of evidence in decision-making and policy. This move recognises that if patients don't accept interventions, they're unlikely to comply with advice about using them.

Check the requirements of your assignments carefully though – not all disciplines favour the inclusion of qualitative research, and some require RCTs and systematic reviews of quantitative research only. If you're not sure about the requirements of your discipline and your specific task, speak to your tutor or supervisor.

Before you choose your topic, make sure you have a clear idea of the specific requirements of your literature review. Here is a checklist with some important points.

Specific requirements	Your notes
Sources	
How many sources do you need to include?	
Any specific instructions about the type of sources you need to include?	
How current do the sources need to be?	
Do you need to use and record systematic techniques for finding and selecting sources?	
Use of gen AI tools	
Are you allowed to use gen AI?	
Are there any specifications about how you can use it and which tools you can use?	
How do you need to record the use of the tools?	
Submission points	
Do you need to submit a question for your review? Due date?	
Do you need to submit a proposal? Due date?	
Do you need to submit a draft? Due date?	
Final date of submission for your literature review?	

2 Choose your topic

Although some literature assignments specify the topic to be reviewed in the literature, many require you to choose a topic for yourself. You may be given a list of topics to choose from, but often you're asked to come up with a topic yourself.

Start with a known area that interests you

If you're doing your review as part of a course, remind yourself about the topics that were covered in workshop slides, videos and recommended readings. What did you find interesting or absorbing? Make a list of two or three possible topics.

Look through core textbooks in your discipline

These textbooks often provide an overview of topic areas in a discipline, and they tend to be conveniently arranged in topic areas, with headings, subheadings and areas of focus, and key terms highlighted in sections.

You can skim through sections to find possible topic areas, then use the key words to do a preliminary search for journal articles and conference papers (see Part 2) to find out what researchers are talking about at the moment.

Subject librarians are often responsible for maintaining **subject guides** on library websites. They can help you find core texts and what researchers are currently talking about by looking at conference proceedings and journal articles in your area of interest. Make an appointment for a consultation.

Keep an eye on what's being discussed in the media

You're looking for topics that are important to society – issues that need answers. News items cover conversations on current topics of interest, and they sometimes refer to recent research that's been done on the topic. You can find the research and pick up the key words to search some more.

Choosing a topic that interests you is a starting point in your literature review journey. Most topics will be too broad to cover in a single project, and you'll need to narrow down your focus to the specific question you want answered from the literature.

This is why tutors often ask you to submit a search question at the start of the process, so that they can provide feedback on whether your question is **answerable** within the word limit of your project and the amount of time you have.

3. Focus your topic into an answerable question

This involves exploratory searching and reading to establish which particular aspect or aspects of the topic interest you. You can then refine the question you want answered from the literature.

Topic of interest (broad)	Answerable question (focused)
Motivation in maths	*How can parents build their children's intrinsic motivation for maths learning through home-based parental involvement?*
Post-traumatic stress syndrome (PTSD) in refugees	*What are the risk factors and most effective interventions for PTSD in resettled women refugees?*
Dance therapy	*What is the evidence on the use of dance therapy for improving mobility in post-stroke patients?*

Even if you're not required to submit a question, it's worth taking the time to formulate one and get feedback. Your question indicates the scope or boundaries of your topic and gives you a specific focus for your literature search so that you can find what you're looking for quickly in the library databases (see p. 40).

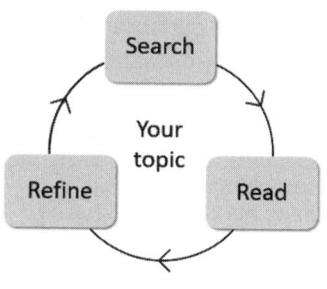

There's a vast amount of literature out there. If you start your search from too broad a topic of interest, you could end up looking through thousands of journal articles and books to find what you need.

As you start reading to refine your topic, you'll pick up the key words and concepts used in your topic area. You can include these words in your search strategy. So a preliminary process of searching, reading and refining can save you a lot of time later.

Which sources can you use to help you refine a topic?

General information sites such as **Wikipedia** offer a great starting point for reading and getting an overview on the topic and related subtopics. Articles often feature key authors and key words you can include to start refining your search of library databases.

Review articles in peer-reviewed journals offer a reliable and often comprehensive overview on a topic – the existing knowledge, gaps and details on future areas for research. These articles generally arrange their reviews into themes and subthemes on a topic so they're easy to search for areas of focus. Review articles also bring together the most important researchers and current research.

 You can also use an article's reference list to find out more about the topic, related subtopics and key authors.

Get strategic about your topic

As you read, asking the six strategic questions can be a really useful way of narrowing your focus in your topic of interest.

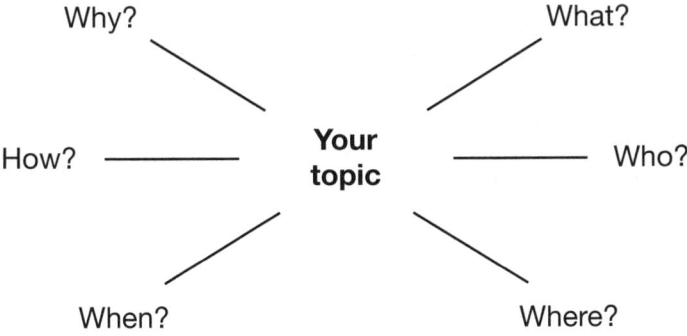

What? (specific aspect of the topic)
Is there a specific aspect, subtopic or issue you find interesting/is seen as particularly important? A specific type or category? A specific cause/effect?

Who? (people/population)
- Age/age group, e.g. early childhood
- Generation, e.g. millennials/gen Z
- Demographic, e.g. minimum wage earners.

Where? (setting/location)
- Physical location, e.g. in the home/classroom/critical care ward
- Geographical location, e.g. country/province or rural/urban
- Virtual spaces, e.g. specific social networking sites/online learning environments

When? (time)
- Span of time, e.g. during the Covid epidemic/in the 1990s/in the last decade
- Period of time, e.g. during the first year of primary school

How? (particular perspective/approach)
Viewing the topic through the lens of a particular theory or approach can help narrow your focus significantly, e.g. from the perspective of Vygotsky's sociocultural theory

Why? (why this focus is important)
You'll need to justify the focus of your literature review, so it's important to ask this question as you start to identify aspects of the topic you find interesting

For example, Anisha's interest in the topic of refugees began with her community practice experience where she discovered that PTSD is often undiagnosed in refugees and can have serious consequences for them and their families. She began to read and narrow her topic:

PTSD among refugees ⟹ What are the risk factors and most effective interventions for PTSD in resettled women refugees?

What? Anisha narrowed her focus to two specific aspects of the problem

Who? She focused on a specific category in refugee populations and on a specific gender

Why? Her preliminary reading revealed that this group is particularly vulnerable to undiagnosed PTSD

Anisha could further narrow her focus by viewing the topic through a specific theory **(How?)**, or by focusing on a specific location **(Where?)**, such as refugees in developed economies or, more specifically, in a particular country.

As you narrow your focus, check whether there's enough literature within the boundaries of the topic to fit the *number* of sources specified for your task and the *type* of sources required.

Be careful of questions that are so narrow they require a factual answer from a single source rather than a review of the literature, such as: How many resettled women refugees are there in New Zealand?

Use a formula to construct your question

You can also use a question formula or model to help you focus your topic into an answerable question for the literature. One of the most widely used in the health sciences is PICO, which identifies four components:

- **P** Problem/population/patient
- **I** Intervention
- **C** Comparison (if there is one)
- **O** Outcome

Sometimes, a C is added for context – 'where' an intervention is happening, or a T for time – 'when' it is happening, such as time of day or duration of intervention.

For many students doing a literature review using a systematic approach, formulating a PICO question is a required first step. **Note:** University library websites provide other frameworks for formulating questions, such as SPIDER, SPICE and ECLIPSE. Some of these may better fit qualitative questions or fields of study.

Karl focused his initial interest in dance therapy to his answerable question:

Dance therapy ➟ What is the evidence on the use of **dance therapy** (Intervention) for **improving mobility** (Outcome) in **post-stroke patients** (Patient/population)?

How can gen AI help me?

Gen AI tools can:

Help you brainstorm ideas for a topic:

Example prompt:
I am a third-year undergraduate student in primary education and I need to complete a 1,500-word literature review on maths learning. Please suggest some interesting and current topics.

Help you narrow or widen your topic:

Example prompt:
Please narrow the scope of the topic: Motivation in maths learning

 Save your chats by copying and pasting them into a Word document. Not all tools save them for you. You might also need a record of your chats, including time and date, to acknowledge the use of gen AI tools in your literature review.

Focus your topic into an answerable question

Chatbots are not always reliable sources of information. You might get information that's not really helpful or may have been made up by the chatbot (called a *hallucination*). If this happens, it's better to stop the chat, revise your prompts, and start a new chat.

It's also important to check with your tutor or supervisor on the suitability of your topic, and make sure it fits with the requirements of your assignment or research topic.

Checklist for your topic	✓
Is it important to know the answer to your question?	
Can the existing literature on the topic answer your question?	
Can the question be answered within the requirements of your literature review task?	

PART 2: FINDING AND SELECTING YOUR SOURCES

From your initial search, you know that researchers are talking about your topic. Now you're ready for a closer look at their conversations to find the key voices that will help you answer your question.

4 Design your search strategy

A search strategy is a set of terms used to search and make decisions around where to search and which search techniques to use. You're going to be moving away from more general search engines like Google, to searching library databases. The content of these databases is regularly monitored to give you access to current, high-quality sources. Searching them efficiently means being clear about:

- What type of sources you're looking for
- Where you're likely to find them
- How to conduct your search.

What types of sources do you need to find?

There will be different requirements about sources depending on your discipline, the type of review you're doing, and your level of study. These are some of the most common types of sources that feature in literature reviews.

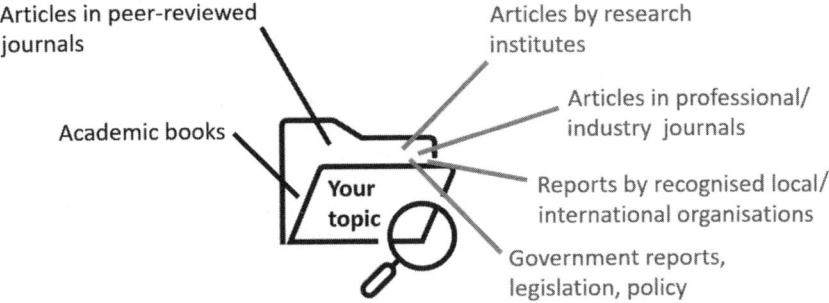

The sources on the left are generally considered to be academic or scholarly sources – written by academics for the academic community. Those on the right are sometimes referred to as 'grey literature' – sources published by experts outside the academic community and not peer-reviewed.

For many literature review tasks, you'll refer to academic literature and 'grey literature' on your topic. Both are legitimate sources of knowledge. These are two of the sources from Anisha's review on PTSD among refugees.

Academic sources example	
Lewis et al. (2020) Psychological therapies for post-traumatic stress disorder in adults: Systematic review and meta-analysis. *European Journal of Psychotraumatology*, 11(1). https://doi.org/10.1080/20008198.2020.1729633	Systematic review articles are considered the gold standard of evidence – the most reliable source of evidence on a topic. This is because they use rigorous search and selection methods to bring together *all* the available evidence to answer a research question. Anisha uses the article to provide evidence on the effectiveness of specific interventions for PTSD.
Grey literature example	
United Nations High Commission for Refugees (2023) *Figures at a glance*. www.unhcr.org/about-unhcr/who-we-are/figures-glance	Anisha uses this report from the UNHCR to define the concept 'refugee' and highlight the importance of her broader topic by providing current refugee numbers worldwide (see p. 122).

Where will you find the sources you need?

The best starting point for your research is normally your university's library catalogue.

This is a way to search all the materials in your library, including academic/professional articles, books, ebooks, dissertations and theses.

You can also search **Google Scholar** for academic/scholarly writing and grey literature. Many of the sources in Google Scholar are not freely available to the public but searching it through your university library gives you access to all the sources in the library databases. It searches for terms related to your key terms as well, so you can get a very large number of sources to sort through.

Google Scholar is a great starting point for your search, but you can't limit your search to peer-reviewed articles, so you'll need to check the individual sources if this is a requirement.

For a more targeted search for evidence, you can use the research databases on your library website.

Research databases

These are online collections of high-quality sources you can access through your university library website. Unlike Google Scholar, they primarily retrieve peer-reviewed publications, such as academic journals, and may include conference papers, books, industry journals and media reports.

Universities subscribe to these databases so that students can use them free of charge. Some databases, such as Academic Search Complete, JSTOR and Scopus, cover a broad range of topics across subject areas, while others target specific subjects.

Library websites provide links to subject guides – web pages that recommend key databases relevant to your subject.

When you open a database, it looks something like this:

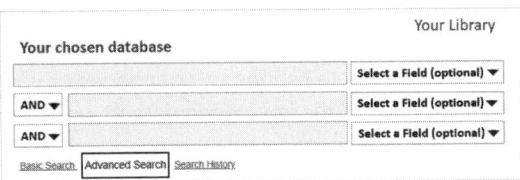

You insert key words from your topic, and the database will search hundreds of sources that combine those key terms.

Features like Advanced Search in many databases allow you to limit the focus of the search (say, by date and publication type), so that you retrieve information that fits the specific requirements of your literature review task and any eligibility criteria you need to apply.

Databases only search for the words you tell them to find, but key words and concepts can be expressed in different ways in sources. So, to make sure you're not missing out on important information relevant to your topic, it's helpful to develop a systematic way of searching databases.

Design your search strategy

5 Search the library databases

You'll be searching across the topic areas that define the scope or boundaries of your question. Begin your search by brainstorming a list of the key concepts and words for your topic.

Brainstorming key search words

You can do an initial search in Google Scholar or library search to collect related search words from articles on your topic.

For example, Karl wants to find out:

What is the evidence on the use of dance therapy for improving mobility in post-stroke patients?

He lists his key words in a table and adds any similar words or phrases he finds in articles.

Key concepts →	dance therapy	post-stroke	mobility
Related search words	dance intervention	stroke	motor activity
	dance	stroke rehabilitation	motor locomotion
		sub-acute stroke	

DOING YOUR LITERATURE REVIEW

He then uses these key words to search for sources in academic databases. He uses the words AND/OR and symbols, known as 'Boolean operators', to create strings of search words.

Words and symbols	Function	Example
AND	Links different key words to narrow your search	therapy **AND** mobility
OR	Searches for similar key words to broaden your search	therapy **OR** intervention
*	Truncates a word – enables searching for different forms of a word	therap* for therapy, therapist, therapeutic
" "	Searches for a phrase	"dance therapy", "motor activity"

Karl then enters his search strings into a database, using an advanced search.

Your Library

Your chosen database

"dance therap*" OR "dance intervention*" OR "dance program*"	Select a Field (optional) ▼
AND ▼ "post-stroke" OR stroke OR "stroke rehabilitation" OR "sub-acute stroke"	Select a Field (optional) ▼
AND ▼ mobility OR "motor activity"	Select a Field (optional) ▼

<u>Basic research</u>   Advanced Search   <u>Search History</u>

Search the library databases

Searching the literature with gen AI

1 You can use a gen AI chatbot to suggest key words for your search:

> **Example prompt:**
> I need to create useful database search strings for my literature review assignment with the topic: "Encouraging intrinsic motivation for maths learning through parental involvement". Please provide me with a list of words I can use.

2 You can also use the free or trial version of AI research tools such as ResearchRabbit and Litmaps to do a search of the literature for you, using
- a key concept, such as dance therapy intervention
- your search strings, such as dance therapy AND post-stroke patients.

These tools commonly use Google Scholar and Semantic Scholar as their databases. You can compare the results with your search of the databases to check for any missing sources in your original database search. These research tools not only give you references and abstracts, they may also provide you with a list of similar publications, often presented in a visual map of connections.

Their output may look something like this:

Search ...	Articles	Visual map / list of related articles	
➤ Create visual map ➤ Create tags (for folders and key concepts)	Author, date Title Journal Number of references Number of citations	*(scatter plot)* Explore related articles	Similar work 1: ✓ Select abstract ... Title etc. Similar work 2: ✓ Select abstract ... Title etc.
	...	...	

CAUTION: Always make sure that sources found by AI are genuine.

A few things you can check:

- Does the article have an author, and can you find the author in a database search?
- Can you find the article title in a Google Scholar search?
- Is the article published in a journal, and can you find the journal?
- Does the article have a digital object identifier (DOI)?

What if I'm not getting the sources or other information I need?

If your search strategies in the library databases do not give you all the information needed, you can change or broaden your key words, using similar concepts or words.

> Therap* OR Intervention OR Treatment
>
> AND
>
> Mobility OR "Motor activity" OR "Motor locomotion" etc.

The 'OR' will broaden your search to include all articles containing one of these concepts.

You can also speak to your lecturer or subject librarian for advice on finding relevant sources.

Recording your search strategy

Tutors will often expect you to keep a record of how you searched the literature. Record everything you do as you do it and the results you get. For a literature review with a systematic methodology, keep detailed notes as you may need to report your search details in a detailed diagram, such as a PRISMA flowchart (see p. 61).

6. Evaluate and select your sources

Your initial search process will probably bring up far more sources than you can use in your literature review. You've chosen an important topic, so it's likely that there will be a lot of voices contributing to the conversation. It's useful to have a system that will help you to select the key voices that will help you to answer your question and meet the requirements of your task.[1]

Using a criteria checklist

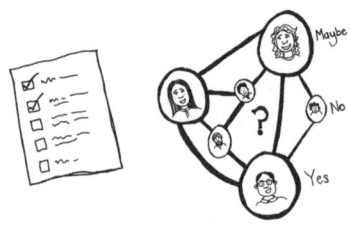

When you find a potential source, you can use a checklist of criteria to help you decide as quickly as possible whether it's worth reading in more detail.

The following table features five commonly used criteria that can be applied to analyse any source, and some questions that can help you consider the worth of the source for inclusion in your literature review.

---

1 See *Getting Critical* in this series for more on evaluating potential sources.

Criteria	You can ask questions concerning:
1 Authority Credibility of the content creator as a source of information on your topic	**Author(s)** What else have they published? Does their name keep coming up in sources? Authors cite the work of prominent researchers, so it's a good indication of someone's authority on the topic. What are their credentials? Are they affiliated with a university, research institute or other reputable organisation? Has your tutor/supervisor mentioned the author? Is their work featured in reading lists, if available, in your courses? If not, check with your subject librarian – they work with teaching staff to create these lists. Course materials tend to feature key authors on topics.
	Organisations If the source was created by an organisation, are they considered to be a trusted and objective authority in the topic area? For example, the World Health Organization, the World Economic Forum, or UNESCO. You can check your library course guide for recommended organisational sites and speak to your subject librarian.

	Publishers If you're looking at a journal article, is the journal peer-reviewed? For a book/book chapter, does it have a reference list? This is more likely to be a scholarly source. Is the journal considered relevant or acceptable for your specific discipline? Sometimes, disciplines value certain journals over others. Speak to your tutor or supervisor if you're not sure. Your subject librarian might also have some insight into this.
2 Accuracy How trustworthy the information is	**Evidence provided** Do the authors provide evidence for claims they make? For example, are there in-text references to sources and details in reference lists? Is the evidence reliable? Does it come from sources with authority such as peer-reviewed journal articles? Is the evidence current? How was the evidence obtained? Does it fit the specifications for your review? For example, does the methodology used in research articles fit the requirements for the types of sources that should be included?

Criteria	You can ask questions concerning:
3 Objectivity The presence of possible bias in the information	**Purpose of author/organisation in creating content** Are they trying to sell you something? Are they trying to persuade you to support their opinion/cause? Often, these types of sources rely on emotional language to persuade the reader, rather than evidence-based argument(s). Is only one perspective on the topic covered, or are other perspectives acknowledged? **Affiliations/background of author** If research has been funded by a private company, could this have affected the information provided? Check for any declarations and disclosures by authors. These are often included in the last pages of journal articles.
4 Currency The timeliness of the information	**Publication dates** When was the source published or last updated? Is it still relevant to your topic/project or is it outdated? As a general rule, sources in the sciences, technology and medicine need to have been published within the last five years to be considered current. Other subject areas such as the social sciences and the humanities may consider five to ten years as current. Check your assignment brief or guidelines for specific currency requirements.

5 Coverage (relevance) The extent to which the content meets your needs	**Your topic** Will it help you answer your question? Which aspects of your topic does it cover? To what extent?

The good news is that you don't have to read through entire sources to make your choice!

Evaluate and select your sources

How do I find the information I need quickly?

The first page of journal articles can provide you with some of the information you need.

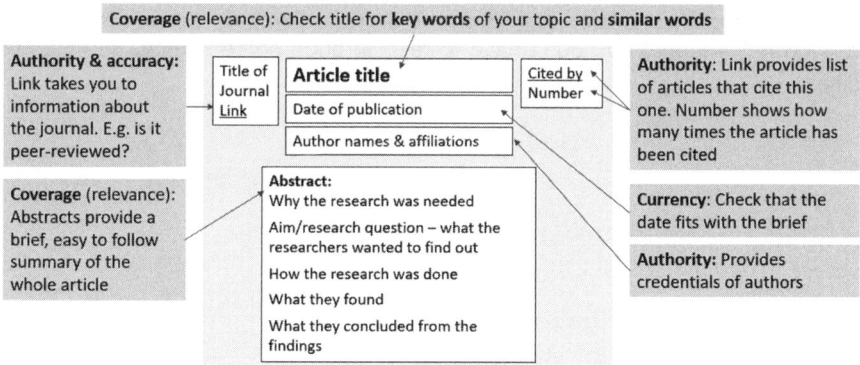

Once you've selected your sources by checking abstracts, you can then dive deeper into an article to assess more thoroughly its usefulness and limitations. Knowing the structure of research articles is helpful for finding the information you need.

Where can I find information in research articles?

Section	Here you can find out:
Introduction	**Which specific conversation is this study entering and why is it important?** This section gives you background information on the topic and evidence of the importance of the researchers' focus.
Literature review	**What are the main issues in this conversation and who's talking about them?** Here, the researchers give an overview of the relevant literature and make it clear to the reader how their research fits in. You'll find key definitions, concepts and related theories; previous findings and debates; and references to the researchers who are discussing all of this.
Methodology	**How did the researchers go about finding out what they wanted to know?** This kind of information might be most useful if you're focusing closely on how the evidence in the study was obtained.
Findings/results	**What did their analysis of the data reveal?** Here, the writers present their results, and often summarise them in table form.

Discussion	**What has this study contributed to the conversation?** Researchers often summarise the most important findings of the study, then interpret and situate them in the previous research on the topic. They also discuss their study's strengths and weaknesses. In this way, they clarify how their research adds to our understanding of the topic.
Conclusions and recommendations	**What's still missing from the conversation?** Here, researchers often emphasise their main contribution to the topic, summarise limitations and make recommendations for further research. This is a great place to find information on gaps in current knowledge and the need for more research.
References	**Who else is taking part in the conversation?** Reference lists can provide a shortcut to more sources with relevant information on your topic – skim through them. They often have active links to relevant sources.

Review articles are structured more like a book chapter or essay. You can skim[2] through the introduction, headings, subheadings and conclusion to check for relevance to your topic.

---

2 See *Where's Your Evidence* in this series for more on skim-reading strategies.

DOING YOUR LITERATURE REVIEW

What if a source doesn't directly address my question?

You'll be searching across the related topic areas that define the scope or boundaries of your question. Researchers in the literature will be having conversations involving some of those topic areas, but within the context of their specific research projects, so they might not directly address your question.

Emma's question on how parents can motivate their children for maths learning involved looking for conversations covering three topic areas, some of them separate and some overlapping. She found journal articles and books or book chapters focusing only on maths learning or motivation, or parental involvement in learning generally. She also found some in which the researchers focused on maths learning and motivation, and some in which they focused on all three areas.

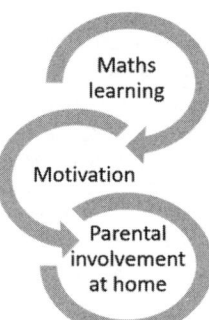

Evaluate and select your sources

The table below has three reference list entries for Emma's assignment on the topic. You can see from the titles of the articles that some make a direct contribution to all three topic areas, while others directly address only one or two of the areas.

Silinskas, G. and Kikas, E. (2019) Parental involvement in math homework: Links to children's performance and motivation. *Scandinavian Journal of Educational Research*, 63(1): 17–37.	This title indicates that the research covers all three topic areas in the assignment. It also covers the issue of homework, which directly addresses Emma's focus on home-based learning
Jay, T., Rose, J. and Simmons, B. (2018) Why is parental involvement in children's mathematics learning hard? Parental perspectives on their role supporting children's learning. *SAGE Open*, April–June, 1–13.	The title indicates that the research covers two of the topic areas in the assignment
Wilder, S. (2014) Effects of parental involvement on academic achievement: A meta-synthesis. *Educational Review*, 66(3): 379–97.	This title indicates that the research covers one of the topic areas and academic achievement in general.

Recording source details and your evaluation notes

When you find a source you think you can use, start recording the publication details and brief notes from your evaluation straight away.[3] You've spent valuable time skimming through potential sources and you don't want to have to repeat this process later on because you've forgotten those initial thoughts! Start your note-making process as early as possible – you can update and extend your notes as you engage more closely with your sources.

 For a large list of sources, start getting familiar with reference management tools, such as EndNote, Zotero and Mendeley. But, before you decide on a tool, check or ask a subject librarian whether you can integrate it with your word processing software, as EndNote only supports Microsoft Word (pc and Mac), while Zotero and Mendeley also support LibreOffice Writer for Linux users.

---

3 See *Where's Your Evidence* in this series for more on recording your evaluation notes

Evaluating the quality of evidence in research studies

Some subjects use specific tools for evaluating sources for inclusion or exclusion in a literature review, especially when it is a systematic review of the literature. For example, CASP (Critical Appraisal Skills Programme) checklists[4] are widely used in the health sciences to evaluate research studies in terms of the quality of the evidence provided.

Each checklist focuses on a specific type of study and uses questions to help you think in a systematic way about how the research was done, and the results generated. Regardless of which subject area you're writing in, CASP checklists can provide a useful starting point for your evaluation of research sources.

---

4 Free downloadable checklists for the different types of studies can be found at: https://casp-uk.net/casp-tools-checklists/

Being objective in your inclusion/exclusion process

When you evaluate sources, avoid choosing only those voices you agree with as it may reflect potential bias on a topic. In contrast, when you include diverse ideas, arguments and findings, it signals that you've approached the literature with curiosity and objectivity – an open mind. Such an approach will later help you write a well-balanced literature review with convincing arguments and insightful conclusion(s) on your topic.

For example, in Andrew's literature review, he includes different theoretical perspectives on his topic before justifying the particular perspective he uses in his research (see his outline on p. 84).

As Professor Alison Jones (2007) commented in her advice on literature reviews: 'Those researchers and writers you refer to in your literature review are those you invite into the conversation. You must invite in your enemies as well as your friends. Only this way will you have a robust conversation!'

Keep going back to your question to avoid lengthy detours

It's easy to get side-tracked by interesting but irrelevant readings in your searching and note-taking. Keep asking: Is this source going to help me answer my question? How? Or is it outside the boundaries of my topic?

How do I know when I've finishing searching?

If no requirements for the number of sources are given, it may be hard to stop searching. For a literature review in a larger project like a dissertation or thesis, it may be helpful to step back and take stock of the process. For example, are you seeing the same sources coming up in other database searches? If so, you're probably done, at least for a while.

You'll often find that as you process your chosen texts and plan and write your review, you're likely to find that there are gaps in your understanding or evidence, and you need to search for additional sources on the topic to address these gaps.

Recording your choices about inclusion or exclusion

Keep in mind that when your literature review is **systematic**, your reading of abstracts, headings and specific sections will help you make decisions according to the selection and criteria protocols you need to incorporate. These protocols commonly provide you with additional questions for assessing the suitability of a source for inclusion.

It is important to make notes about your decisions. You often need to report the databases you accessed, and your criteria for selection and exclusion in the method section. You may include a visual decision chart like PRISMA,[5] and a description of the eligibility criteria and process.

> An article's eligibility was based on the following criteria: … This was followed by conducting an itemised relevance check to rate an article's degree of relevance for … The article was given a low relevance rating if it only described … but failed to discuss …

Note: Increasingly, tutors and supervisors now require you to explain briefly the search and selection process in a paragraph as part of all types of literature reviews.

---

5 You can download flowchart documents for new and updated systematic reviews at: www.prisma-statement.org/prisma-2020-flow-diagram

PART 3
READING AND MAKING NOTES

When you've found quality sources that will help you answer your question, you can engage more deeply with their content.[6] You've been critical in selecting them; now, you also need to be critical in analysing their contribution to understanding on your topic.

Your reader wants more than just a list or summary of what each source says on your topic. They want a *response* to the sources – *your perspective* on their contributions and how they fit together to answer your question.

---

6 See *Reading and Making Notes* in this series

You're aiming for this:	**Not this:**
Argument presenting evaluation, comparison and synthesis of a range of sources in response to a question ☺	Largely descriptive account of individual sources on topic ☹

It's easy to slip into just describing what your sources say in a literature review, but a way of making sure you stay on track is to consciously engage with your sources as you read and use a note-taking system that records this engagement.

7. Engage with your sources

This means that you're not passively taking in what each source says. Instead, you're actively engaging with the content by asking questions as you read to reflect on the meaning for your topic, and how you might use the information to answer your question.

Building on what you know

Reading and understanding is a cumulative process. You've already developed some ideas about the topic from what others have said – your tutors, media coverage, your own experience, and your skim-reading process in selecting your sources.

Now you can start deepening your understanding and developing your own perspective on the topic by reflecting on how the content in your selected sources fits in with these conversations and with each other.

As you read, you can use what you already know to understand, evaluate and compare the contribution of your sources to understanding on your topic.

Making notes as you read

As you start reading more closely, three questions can help you summarise and reflect on sources:[7]

1 **What** is the source saying?
   - Book chapter: What is the main argument and how is it supported? What does the author conclude?
   - Research article: What was the aim of the research? How was it conducted? What were the findings relevant to your topic? What did the authors conclude from the findings?

2 **So what** are the implications for your topic?
   - Does it add to your understanding? How?
   - Does it challenge your understanding/suggest you need further understanding on some aspect of the topic?
   - What's still missing? What are the gaps/limitations identified?
   - How does it compare with information from your other sources? Does it agree/disagree? Is it inconclusive?

3 **What now?**
   - Where and how do you think you might use the information in your review?
   - Is there any further information you need to find?

---

7 See *Planning Your Dissertation and Getting Critical* in this series for more on reflecting on sources

There are various formats you can use to take notes using questions like these. You can make notes on hard copies of articles or online documents you can access anywhere. Choose a note-taking system you are comfortable using and that allows you to move backwards and forwards between entries quickly and easily to add information.[8] We'll suggest a few possibilities.

Annotated bibliography

This is a list of references for sources, with annotations (brief notes) about each source. Tutors and supervisors sometimes ask students to submit one of these to check on their progress with reading for their literature review.

Below is an extract from Anisha's annotated bibliography with notes on a source for her review on risk factors and interventions for PTSD in women refugees. She uses the 'What', 'So what' and 'What now' questions to guide her annotations (see highlighted words).

---

8 See also Chapters 11 and 12 of *Where's Your Evidence* in this series

Publication details	Im, H. and Swan, L.E. (2021) Working towards culturally responsive trauma-informed care in the refugee settlement process: Qualitative inquiry with refugee-serving professionals in the United States. *Behavioural Sciences*, **11(11): 155.** https://doi.org/10.3390/bs11110155
1. What? Description of what was done, how, & relevant findings	Interviewed 78 individual refugee service providers in the US on adaptation of trauma-informed care (TIC) in refugee resettlement programmes. Found awareness of resettlement stressors and trauma triggers for new refugees + support for ITC care BUT challenges from lack of (1) training & inexperience in provision of TIC adaptation for refugees (2) culturally responsive knowledge & practices (3) opportunity & time for interagency & community knowledge sharing.
2. So what? Contribution to understanding Comparison with other sources & theories Evaluation in terms of topic boundaries	Provides insights into effectiveness of TIC from perspective of providers. Highlights current limitations of care for refugees in transcultural context. Similar to findings from Wylie et al (2018) – barriers to communication & trust due to lack of knowledge about issues re cultural safety & perceptions of illness. Supports findings by Hawkins (2021) re need for collaboration & community engagement for better outcomes. Aligns with Ryan et al.'s psychological model (2008) & socio-ecological theory. Strength for topic: Focuses on resettled refugees. Limitation: focuses on all refugee groups & doesn't provide any specific insights from women but useful evidence about TIC.
3. What now? Possible use in lit review & further info needed	Could be used in argument that although TIC is accepted as important frontline care for PTSD there are challenges (barriers?) with refugees in terms of implementation. Check for qualitative evidence from refugee perspective (particularly women).

Engage with your sources

As you deepen your understanding of your topic, you can keep adding to and changing your notes. If you're doing a larger project such as a dissertation, an annotated bibliography can serve as a record of your changing thinking on the topic.

Multiple source reading grid

A reading grid can help you to record information from multiple sources. In the example below, the columns indicate specific aspects of research, and each row can record notes from one source. The student has added a column at the end for their comments on how they might use the source. You can change the column headings according to your research focus or task.

Your topic:

	Topic/question	Methodology	Findings	Limitations	Areas for future research	Comments
Source 1						
Source 2						
Source 3						

A reading grid like this allows you to see similarities and differences between information in your sources at a glance. You can use a spreadsheet like Excel for an extensive literature review.

Do I need to make detailed notes for every source I use?

It depends how much detail from the source you're likely to include in your literature review.

How closely is the source related to your topic?

Sources that directly address your topic may be discussed in more detail in your literature review. For example, if you're doing a research project, you'll want to identify what previous research close to yours has contributed to the topic, and the limitations of their contribution – the gap(s) left that you will fill with your own research (see, for example, p. 103). So, you'll need detailed notes from these sources.

Does your review require a limited number of sources?

In some undergraduate courses, the purpose of a literature review assignment is to assess whether you can find and synthesise evidence from a limited number of journal articles (maybe three to four) that use specific research methodologies. In this case, you're most likely to make detailed notes from all your selected articles to provide extensive detail about each of them in your review.

Are you required to use systematic techniques?

Reviews using systematic techniques often include quite extensive detail from sources in their critical appraisal of existing research (see Karl's assignment on p. 110). Here again you would need extensive notes, often in a specified format. In some cases, your tutor might require you to submit your notes for feedback as a preliminary step to writing the review.

Engage with your sources

Reading and note-making with gen AI

You can prompt a gen AI tool to help you understand difficult texts by explaining complex ideas, concepts or theories in simpler terms.

> **Example prompt**
> *Please explain the concept of globalisation in a way that is easy for a secondary school student to understand.*

CAUTION

Although chatbots can also help you with:

- identifying the key points in a reading
- providing a more visual organisation of a reading
- 'translating' a reading into easy to understand English or other language

uploading any published material to a gen AI tool could mean that you're breaching copyright law.

Managing your references and notes

Reference management tools like Endnote, Zotero or Mendeley can help you organise your readings and notes. Their use of AI technology makes it increasingly possible to:

- tag and organise sources and files in folders according to key concepts or issues
- store abstracts and accessible PDFs from multiple databases into a folder
- annotate text and attach notes.

They also help you keep all your information safe. Your references and notes are:

- 'portable' (stored in the cloud) and accessible on multiple devices
- automatically backed up and synchronised across devices.

PART 4
PLANNING YOUR LITERATURE REVIEW

Once you've made your notes, it's important to take the time to sit back and make sense of how the information from your sources fits together to answer your question.

Catch your breath and consider what's gone before and where you're heading. Go back to the purpose of your review and the requirements (Part 1). Work through your notes describing and evaluating what your sources have contributed to understanding on your topic, and how they relate to each other (Part 3).

Start making sense of how it all fits together: you're now moving towards **synthesising** the information into your arguments on the topic.

> **Synthesise:** Bring together different sources to serve an argument or idea you are constructing. Make logical connections between the different sources that help you shape and support your ideas (The Open University, 2025).

A first step is working out how you can group information from your source into themes and subthemes on your topic.

8. Identify themes and subthemes

In a literature review, **themes** are the main ideas or issues that you identify in your analysis of the literature on your topic. They are categories of information on your topic. **Subthemes** are specific aspects of the main themes – groupings of findings related to the main themes.

As you look back through your readings and notes, identify the key ideas, concepts, events or topics that keep coming up in conversations between researchers. These themes will help you to organise the information in your literature review. They are like umbrellas under which you develop your arguments on specific related aspects.

Mapping major themes

You can use a piece of A3 paper with sticky notes or a virtual whiteboard if you have access to one. In the centre, put the question you need to answer in your literature review.

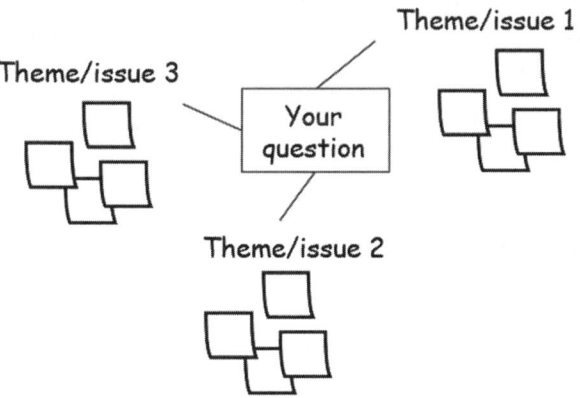

As you identify recurring themes/issues, give them names. Theme names often feature concepts that are central to your topic. Group notes from your sources under each theme, and check that each theme addresses your question.

In the example below, Emma identifies three major themes that answer her question.

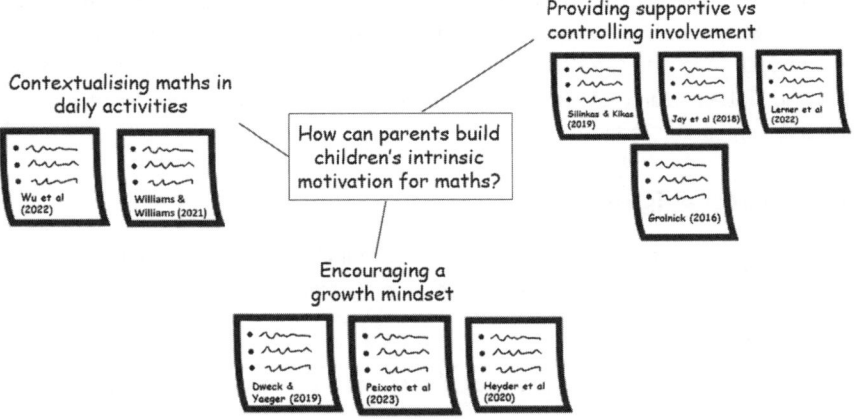

As you bring together your sources, you'll start noticing patterns in the notes that suggest groupings of related issues (subthemes) and you can start adding these as branches to your themes.

You're also likely to find that something you've identified as a theme ends up being a subtheme of something else and you end up with fewer themes. Mapping your themes and subthemes is an iterative process where you keep moving back and forward between your map and the notes. It's part of getting to grips with the complexities of your topic. Take pictures of any changes to your map as a record in case you want to go back to an earlier version.

Using a synthesis matrix

A synthesis matrix is a table that helps you bring together information from your sources for a visual comparison of how they relate to each other.

Your question:

	Source 1	Source 2	Source 3	Source 4	Source 5
Theme/issue 1					
Theme/issue 2					
Theme/issue 3					

Emma's notes might look like this:

How can parents build children's intrinsic motivation for maths?

Sources →	Silinkas & Kikas (2019)	Dweck & Yaeger (2019)	Wu et al (2022)	Oh et al (2023)	Williams & Williams (2021)	Peixoto et al (2023)
Providing supportive vs controlling involvement	~~~		~~~	~~~	~~~	~~~
Encouraging a growth mindset		~~~				~~~
Contextualising maths in daily activities			~~~		~~~	~~~

(First column label: *Major themes*)

Arguments and findings from sources are often spread across themes in a literature review. A table like this helps you to map where they fit in, and where they agree and disagree.

Later in her literature review, Emma synthesises similar findings from the sources in the first row:

> A number of studies have found that perceptions of controlling parental involvement in maths homework appear to inhibit children's intrinsic motivation (Oh et al., 2020; Peixoto et al., 2023; Silinkas & Kikas, 2019).

Identify themes and subthemes

9 Plan the structure of your review

Detailed planning allows you to see the big picture of your review, evaluate your organisation of the information, and make any big changes *before* you start writing. A great way to do this is by creating an outline of your review.

Creating an outline for your themes and subthemes

Once you've identified your themes and subthemes, you can use your notes to start making sense of how you'll organise the information from your sources to provide an answer to your question.

Creating an outline can help you plan your notes into a logical structure. You can use the 'Style option' in MS Word to create different levels of headings for your themes and subthemes: Level 1, level 2 etc. This creates an outline[9] something like the two examples below.

---

[9] In MS Word, you tick the Navigation Pane in 'View' to see headings on the left side of the document

Example 1: Critical review

Anisha's critical review on PTSD in resettled women needs to address the risk factors and interventions for this group. Notice how the headings and subheadings she's used answer the first part of her question:

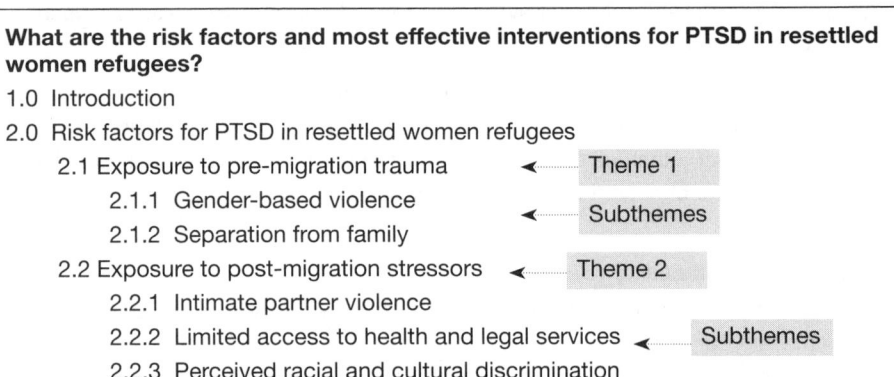

At a glance, the reader can see Anisha's perspective on the major risk factors for women refugees. Undergraduate students might not be expected to use three levels of headings, as per the example above.

Numbering and indenting themes and subthemes in an outline like this helps you to visualise how you'll organise the information in your literature review in a way that makes sense to you and facilitates your arguments about the evidence.

In Anisha's case, it makes sense that she discusses risk factors first because the findings will inform her analysis of available interventions later. She also discusses the most important of those risk factors first.

You can expand your outline to include bullets of the points you want to make in each of your themes and subthemes, and references for the sources you'll use to support them. If you find any themes or subthemes that don't address your question, this is a good time to either change them or leave them out.

Having a detailed outline will allow you to:
- ✓ check that your argument flows logically through your themes and subthemes to answer your question
- ✓ pick up problems before you start writing; e.g., not enough evidence to support a particular argument, so you need to go back to the literature and find more
- ✓ look at the spread of sources: Have you overused a particular source? Is there a reason you need to use it so often?

- ✓ find problems with how you've grouped information under headings and subheadings, or that you've repeated information across themes
- ✓ avoid deleting and relocating (and possibly losing!) a whole lot of information once you've started writing.

Example 2: Literature leading to research questions

The purpose of this kind of review is to situate your research in the existing literature and create a space for your own research. In the social sciences, this often involves explaining and justifying your chosen theoretical perspective on your topic, and the specific model that will guide your research. You then analyse research findings within the focus of this framework to lead the reader to your research questions.

Andrew's research focus is on the transition of elite athletes to retirement. The outline of his literature review chapter shows a clear general to specific organisational pattern as he establishes his framework for the reader.

- 2.0 Introduction
- 2.1 Elite athletes ← *Defines main concepts*
- 2.2 Retirement from elite-level sport ←
- 2.3 Athletic retirement: Theories and models ← *Discusses strengths and limitations of existing theories and models on topic*
- 2.4 Athletic retirement as a transition ←
- 2.5 Framework for the present study ← *Explains & justifies chosen theoretical perspective ... and the use of a related model*
- 2.5.1 Stage 1 – Reasons for athletic retirement
- 2.5.2 Stage 2 – Mediating factors influencing athletes' adjustments to retirement
- 2.5.3 Stage 3 – Available resources for adaptation to retirement ← *Critically analyses previous research findings within framework of chosen model*
- 2.5.4 Stage 4 – Quality of the career transition for elite athletes
- 2.5.5 Stage 5 – Interventions
- 2.6 Summary ← *Draws evidence-based conclusions about need for own research*

Other ways of organising the body of your literature review

While themes and subthemes are a common organisational pattern for the body of a literature review, there are other patterns that might be better suited to the focus of your topic.

Methodological organisation

If the focus of your literature review is on the methodologies used in research, you might organise your review according to the different methodologies, such as qualitative, quantitative and so on.

Chronological structure

In a chronological structure, the literature is arranged in a timeline to analyse how an approach, concept or practice has evolved in a field of study. Instead of themes, your sections can consist of periods of time. You can label them to capture the essence of the ideas, debates and studies that contributed to development at that time.

For example, Josta uses a chronological approach to illustrate the historical development of one of her key topics of research: globalisation. She situates globalisation according to time periods to highlight old and more recent concepts of globalisation.

> 2.1 Globalisation as Early Spread of Human Migration, World Religions and Pre-modern Empires
> 2.2 Globalisation as European Expansion
> 2.3 Globalisation as Paradox: Rise of the Nation State and Spread of Industrial Capitalism
> 2.4 Globalisation as a Recent Phenomenon: Retraction of the Nation State
> 2.5 Globalisation as 'Nothing New': Cyclic Pattern of Globalisation

For literature review assignments, you may also be required to use a format specified by your tutor or school. Check your assignment brief for instructions on required formats and any sample reviews provided.

PART 5: WRITING YOUR LITERATURE REVIEW

10 Drafting your literature review

You're in control of all the voices you bring together in the review – like the conductor of a choir. You make the decisions about how you group individual voices together; how you assign them to parts; how much space you give them in these parts; and how the parts function together to answer the question for your reader.

You're analysing the literature to create something new and useful – **your** perspective on the current state of knowledge on your topic. So, your voice must be the loudest of all.

Here, we focus more closely on synthesising the evidence from your sources into arguments on your topic.

What are arguments in a literature review?

Your arguments are the claims you make about the literature on your topic, supported by evidence from your sources. You're interpreting the evidence for the reader – they want to know what **you** have to say about it. Once you've organised the evidence into themes/issues on your topic, you need to share your insights into how it all fits together and the conclusions you've reached.

So where do you start? The first step involves taking a closer look at how the pieces of evidence compare and start drawing some tentative conclusions. Below is a summary of Andrew's research findings from two studies that examined the issue of pre-retirement planning as a coping skill for helping elite athletes adapt to retirement. Compare the findings and see if you can identify one or two similar findings.

Pre-retirement planning

Alfermann et al. (2004) surveyed 256 former male and female amateur elite athletes from Lithuania, Russia and Germany. They found that pre-planned retirement contributed to improved cognitive, emotional and behavioural adaptation. High athletic identity was linked to poor adjustment. German athletes experienced more positive than negative emotions after retirement compared to Lithuanian and Russian athletes. Stanbulova et al. (2007) surveyed 157 French and Swedish former amateur elite athletes. They found that the transition out of elite sport is a dynamic, multidimensional, multi-level and multi-factor process in which nationality/culture plays an important role. Pre-planned retirement contributed to better adjustment.

Andrew could reach two tentative conclusions:

Pre-retirement planning

Alfermann et al. (2004) surveyed 256 former male and female amateur elite athletes from Lithuania, Russia and Germany. They found that pre-planned retirement contributed to improved cognitive, emotional and behavioural adaptation. High athletic identity was linked to poor adjustment. German athletes experienced more positive than negative emotions after retirement compared to Lithuanian and Russian athletes. Stanbulova et al. (2007) surveyed 157 French and Swedish former amateur elite athletes. They found that the transition out of elite sport is a dynamic, multidimensional, multi-level and multi-factor process in which nationality/culture plays an important role. Pre-planned retirement contributed to better adjustment.

> **So** pre-planning seems to help athletes adjust

> **and** nationality/culture seems to play a role

These are ideas for two possible claims on the issue of retirement pre-planning. Now he needs to look at the bigger picture of related evidence in the literature to construct his arguments.

For example, if he's going to develop an argument that pre-planning seems to help athletes adjust to retirement, his reader will want to know:

- **What** is pre-planning for retirement in this context? (Define the concept)
- **Why/how** does it help? (Provide reasons to support your argument)
- **So what** are the implications for your topic?

Synthesising evidence into arguments

Arguments are generally structured into one main idea per paragraph, beginning with the conclusion you've reached from the evidence. You then support this conclusion by bringing together (synthesising) enough evidence from your sources to provide a persuasive argument.

Below is a paragraph from Andrew's literature review showing his first argument about pre-retirement planning for athletes.

Pre-retirement planning

Pre-retirement planning appears to foster positive adjustment to retirement for elite athletes (Alfermann et al., 2004; Cecic-Erpic et al., 2004; Stambulova et al., 2007). Pre-retirement planning for post-sport life includes psychological planning, financial planning (Taylor & Ogilvie, 2004) and vocational planning (Cecic-Erpic, 2004). Pre-planning for retirement helps elite athletes to reduce their athletic identify prior to retiring (Cecic-Erpic et al., 2004; Lally, 2007; Lawrence, 2004; Stambulova, 1994). This improves their cognitive, behavioural and emotional readiness for post-retirement life (Alfermann et al., 2004; Fortunato & Marchant, 1999; Park et al., 2013; Taylor & Ogilvie, 1994). Consequently, psychologists recommend pre-retirement planning (e.g. life skills programmes) during elite athletes' sport careers (Carr & Bauman, 1996; Millet & Kerr, 2002).

Annotations:
- Main point – conclusion reached about evidence
- Clarification/definition of concept
- Supporting evidence for argument – reasons for perceived benefit
- Implications for topic & link to next main idea

Andrew's paragraph provides what is often described in marking guides as a:

> Synthesis of evidence from a range of sources to present coherent arguments on topic

Grouping of references

As part of synthesising evidence on the topic, references to sources providing information on the same point are often grouped, rather than shown separately:

- **In a single reference bracket to show agreement in the evidence:**

    Pre-retirement planning appears to foster positive adjustment to retirement for elite athletes (Alfermann et al., 2004; Cecic-Erpic et al., 2004; Stambulova et al., 2007).

- **Across a sentence to provide evidence on related aspects of a single point:**

    Pre-retirement planning for post-sport life includes psychological planning, financial planning (Taylor & Ogilvie, 2004) and vocational planning such as career planning (Cecic-Erpic, 2004).

- **Across sentences to show similar or contrasting results in research:**

  Research has linked teachers' autonomy-supportive practices with higher maths achievement (Wang et al., 2020; Wei et al., 2017). **However**, the same link has not been established between autonomy-supportive homework involvement by parents (Retanal, 2021).

In these examples, the focus is on the information provided, so the authors' names are placed in reference brackets at the end of the information. But sometimes you may want to provide the details of a particular study; for example, if it provides notable and convincing evidence on an aspect of your topic. In that case, the name of the researcher(s) often becomes part of the sentence. Compare the references in this extract.

Studies grouped to highlight similarities in findings	Perceived controlling practices by parents have been linked with lower levels of intrinsic motivation and maths achievement in children (Oh et al., 2022; Silinkas & Kikas, 2019).
A recent study with a notable and convincing finding on the topic	Furthermore, recent research from Peixoto et al. (2024) suggests that this link could be consistent across cultures. The researchers used data collected from 287 schools and surveys of parents across six European countries to examine the association between parental beliefs and involvement and their children's motivation and achievement in maths learning. They found that …

You may also want to include the name of a researcher(s) in a sentence if you want to draw attention to their name or names. This might be because they are prominent voices in your topic area. For example, they may have done groundbreaking research on your topic, or they may have come up with a well-known theory.

Language for discussing similarities and differences in research

Writers use phrases to signal to the reader their intention to discuss similarity and difference.

Signalling similarity	Signalling difference
This finding is consistent with previous research which showed that …	This finding does not support previous research …
Similarly, …	In contrast, …
These findings align with/support …	
Some researchers have argued …	However, others have pointed out that …
Several studies have reported …	While some studies have reported … others have found that …
There is a general consensus in the research that …	However, researchers differ in their interpretations of …

These signals also help to create 'flow' in the writing by connecting information.

Creating 'flow' in your writing

In writing that flows, ideas are logically organised and clearly connected to guide the reader through your arguments, from section to section, paragraph to paragraph, and sentence to sentence. We've highlighted the connecting words in the extract below.

Links to discussion in previous section	**Despite the prevalence of mental health problems among resettled women refugees,** their ongoing psychosocial needs remain a neglected area in research and policy (Mundy et al. 2020; Vallejo-Martin et al. 2021). Ethical concerns that data collection processes could retraumatise participants by triggering traumatic content have presented barriers to ethical approval for research with resettled refugees (Matos et al., 2023; Vallejo-Martin et al. 2021). **However,** researchers have argued that excluding refugees from research due to their
Presents main point for this paragraph	
Provides reason as supporting point	
Signals **counter-argument**	

> vulnerabilities further disenfranchises them (Matos et al., 2021). **Furthermore,** excluding them constitutes a violation of the ethical codes of justice and fairness since the research can inform targeted evidence-based interventions to improve outcomes for this group (Seagle et al., 2020).
>
> **One of the limitations of current research on refugee women** is that it has not sufficiently captured their diverse experiences of the resettlement process.

*Signals **further** counter-argument* (points to "Furthermore,")

***Links** to related point in new paragraph* (points to "One of the limitations...")

Getting critical about the existing research on your topic

Being critical about the literature on your topic does not mean criticising researchers and their studies. It means discussing the contribution of research to understanding on your topic (both strengths and limitations) and indicating where more research is needed (gaps in the research).

Highlighting the value of a theoretical perspective

In your review of the literature, you might focus on a particular theoretical perspective. This is like a lens through which you view the literature on your topic. You need more than just a description of the theory. In this extract, Emma explains **why** a specific theory is valuable for her review on parental involvement and maths learning.

Highlights value of the theory for the review by providing a reason

Further explains relevance to review

> Given its focus on specific social-contextual factors that can facilitate or undermine motivation, Ryan and Deci's Self-determination Theory (SDT) (2000) **provides a useful framework for** explaining the impact of parental involvement on motivation in maths learning. As the primary socialising agents of their children, parents create day-to-day contexts which can determine the degree to which children's needs for competence, autonomy and relatedness are satisfied in several domains of their lives, including education (Grolnick, 2016) …

Highlighting gaps/limitations in the research

Sometimes the conclusion you'll reach after comparing related research is that more evidence is required on an issue. Here, Andrew notes a finding on possible national/cultural differences from a study, and concludes that more evidence is required on the topic.

> Stambulova et al. (2007) reported that higher numbers of French (55%) and Swedish (67%) elite athletes pre-plan their retirement. A possible explanation for this is that most Western Europeans are from individualist cultures that tend to prioritise planning and are thus more likely to pre-plan for retirement (Stambulova et al., 2009; Triandis, 2004). Cross-cultural differences can potentially influence whether elite athletes pre-plan for retirement; **however, further research is needed to clarify this** ...

- Identifies notable finding related to theme
- Suggests a culture-related explanation, supported by evidence from literature
- Concludes that culture could be a factor, but more research is required

Highlighting gaps/limitations in the research is an important part of your literature review. You're not only presenting arguments about what **is** known about the topic, but also what **is not yet** known or understood. You might be pointing out the need for further research by others, or you may be justifying the gap for your own research.

Presenting arguments about limitations in current understanding

You're showing the reader that you have a grasp of the big picture of the literature on your topic. This often involves making overview statements about the body of existing research. In the extract below, Anisha points out the lack of qualitative research on her topic and why this limitation matters. We've highlighted the overview phrases she uses in her argument.

Drafting your literature review

One of the limitations of current research on resettled women refugees is that **it has not sufficiently captured** their diverse experiences of the resettlement process. As Watter (2022) points out, **much of the research has focused on** quantifying the pre-migration trauma experiences of refugees. **The importance of insights** from women's individual narratives before, during and after resettlement **has only recently begun to be addressed in research** (e.g. Borges, 2023). **Further qualitative research is needed to provide** a deeper understanding of the specific stressors influencing women's mental health in their resettlement journeys (Borrocks et al., 2022). **Furthermore, qualitative research can inform** understanding of how personal and sociocultural resilience factors can mitigate these stressors to result in better outcomes for women (Shishehgar et al., 2017).

Presents main argument about existing research on problem

Supports argument by pointing out the **dominant focus** of past research

Signals alignment with new move towards qualitative research …

and presents **reasons** why this research needed to address the problem

Highlighting a specific gap to justify your own research

For example, in the rationale for his research on the experiences of athletes retiring from elite sport, Andrew draws on a study close to his own, and provides a sequence of reasons why his research is needed.

> **Previous research has shown that this is an important issue because ...**
>
> In 2011, the New Zealand Rugby Players Association (NZRPA) surveyed 123 former professional male rugby players (retired since 1996) regarding their retirement experiences; the findings were alarming. Analysis revealed that 72% experienced negative effects (such as depression, feelings of despair, lack of self-esteem, anxiety) within three months of retiring.
>
> **and this is what we do know from the research on the issue**
>
> Some variables, including high athletic identity, were linked with participants struggling to adapt to the transition.
>
> **but what we don't know yet is ...**
>
> **However, it is unclear whether/how** other prominent variables such as perceived control over the decision to retire and coping skills ... affected the outcome of the study.

> **so** further research is required and it's important **because** **In-depth exploration** regarding the influence of such variables on the retirement transition for elite New Zealand athletes **is required as this will potentially** support the development of strategies to help athletes cope better.

Language for signposting gaps/limitations in the research

Signalling gaps …	and a need for further research
However, it is unclear whether/how …	Therefore, further exploration of the problem is required to determine whether …
One of the limitations of current knowledge on this issue is …	Further investigation could provide insights into …
Much of the research has tended to focus on … rather than …	Thus, there is a need for …
However, there are few studies which examine …	Therefore, this exploratory study aims to provide further insights into …

Morley's *Academic phrasebank* (2023) includes more phrases to use in writing about the literature.

Indicating the strength of evidence on your topic

You can also show your critical voice in the language you use to talk about the evidence on your topic. Compare the conclusions drawn about the two interventions below. Which one indicates a higher level of certainty about the evidence?

> Research has demonstrated the effectiveness of trauma-focused therapies as frontline interventions for PTSD in adult refugees.

> Recent research has provided promising evidence of the potential for dance therapy to contribute to enhanced motor function when combined with standard rehabilitation therapy.

Did you pick the first one? The writer's use of the verb 'demonstrated' in this sentence indicates a high level of certainty about the evidence in the research.

> Research **has demonstrated the effectiveness of** trauma-focused therapies as frontline interventions for PTSD in adult refugees.

On the other hand, in the second sentence the writer adds the qualifier 'promising' to the word evidence, and talks about the 'potential' for the therapy to contribute to improved mobility for the patient. The language used is cautious, suggesting a lot less confidence about the evidence.

> Recent research has **provided promising evidence of the potential for** dance therapy to contribute to enhanced motor function when combined with standard rehabilitation therapy.

More subtle language markers

Often you can show your critical voice in the way you talk about a specific finding or argument. For example, Josta uses certain **reporting verbs** and **qualifiers** to show the strong critical voice expected in her discipline when evaluating the readings.

Evaluative language:

In this context, **assume** indicates that Josta is contesting this view	... neoliberal globalists **assume that** globalisation is a novel event, largely driven by expanding, open markets worldwide. Others have shown that globalisation involves many drivers. Shaw (1997) may come closest to a **workable theory** ... Although Shaw's view tends **to overlook** the cultural influences of non-Western civilisations, it **avoids** the **myopic** view that globalisation has no historical precedent but marks a rupture from previous developments. This is not the case; as Faulconbridge and Beaverstock (2008) **argued convincingly** in their article, globalisation is 'an ongoing syndrome' ...
She goes on to discuss a view she aligns with, using **workable** to give it a positive evaluation	
She acknowledges a limitation of this view with **tends to overlook**, and then confirms her alignment by highlighting how it **avoids** the narrow **myopic** view ...	
and provides a supportive argument indicating the strength of the argument with **convincingly**.	

Drafting your literature review

Language markers for reporting, supporting or challenging authors' arguments and findings

Type of language	Confidence	Neutrality	Doubt
Reporting verbs: for accurate meaning, check surrounding text	argue, emphasise, show, assert, reject, refute, confirm, recommend, validate, establish	state, describe, explain, indicate, explore, assess, report, examine	suggest, postulate, posit the view that, imply, hypothesise, believe, assume, claim
Qualifiers: adding a degree of certainty to a word	certainly, definitely, undoubtedly, strongly, firmly, confidently		may/might, slight, doubtful, perhaps, unlikely, possibly, probably, seemingly
Quantifiers: adding a measure or quantity to a word	many, numerous, most(ly), abundant, sufficient, significant, positive, plenty, substantial	several, some	few, little, single, insufficient, seldom, insignificant, sparse, minor, limited, less, hardly, rarely
Evaluative words: providing a value or judgement on what is described	comprehensive, valid, useful, solid, persuasive, thorough, effective convincing, vital	standard, fair	ineffective, unclear, problematic, debatable, superficial, unconvincing

Evaluating how evidence was obtained

In literature reviews in the health sciences, there tends to be a close focus on how researchers have collected their data in studies.

Karl's literature review assignment requires him to focus on the type and quality of evidence provided in his chosen studies, rather than on main themes/issues in the research. This involves:

- describing each study in some detail to capture the most important features to be evaluated for that specific type of study
- evaluating the study in terms of those features
- synthesising the evidence from his chosen studies to answer his question.

Karl organises the body of his literature review into three main sections: quantitative evidence, qualitative evidence and a synthesis of the evidence to answer his question. In the brief extract from his assignment, we've highlighted phrases that show his critical voice.

Brief introduction to section with evaluative comment about body of research

Description of aim, methods, participants, and findings: **Who, what, where, when, how, why**. Details that will be used to evaluate how the evidence was obtained

Quantitative evidence on dance therapy after stroke

A **limited number** of quantitative studies have assessed the impact of dance therapy when combined with standard rehabilitation therapy after stroke…

Bruyneel et al. (2023) conducted a randomised controlled trial (RCT) to assess the effects of a six week dance intervention program on patients' motor recovery after stroke… Sixteen subacute stroke patients were randomly assigned to either a dance group (DG) or a control group (CG) group… The Mini-BESTest, Functional Independence Measure (FIM)… were used to measure… Participants undergoing the dance therapy programme demonstrated an improvement in balance, coordination, and functional independence.

Evaluative comments based on details of how study was conducted →	The randomised assignment of participants and the use of standardised measures helped to reduce bias in the study. **However**, the relatively small sample size due to premature termination of the study means that **the findings must be treated with caution**…
Comparison with next study in section →	The results **are supported in** research by Lee et al. 2020)…

Leading the reader through your themes and subthemes

Each theme and its sub-themes function as a section of the body of your literature review, almost like a mini-essay:

Sample theme and subtheme structure	
Introduce theme	- Explain the theme and its link with your topic - Provide a brief overview of the related subthemes
Develop arguments on subthemes	- Define each subtheme - Present your main argument on the subtheme - Support your argument with evidence
Present conclusions	- Explain significance of findings on theme - Look ahead to the next theme

On the next page is a sample extract from Anisha's first theme:

	2.1 Exposure to pre-migration trauma
Explains theme & its link with broader topic	Refugees are often exposed to highly traumatic events prior to leaving their home countries, and in the process of flight to other countries (Borges, 2023). Cases of extreme violence and loss of family are widely reported in the literature on the pre-migration journey of resettled refugees and are associated with increased risk of developing PTSD (Bogic et al., 2015; Bryant et al., 2023).
Provides overview of subthemes	For women refugees, exposure to gender-based violence during armed conflict and transit experiences presents significant risks, particularly when combined with separation from family and community.
	2.1.1 Gender-based violence
Defines first subtheme Presents main argument Provides supporting evidence	A widely used definition of gender-based violence (GBV) is that it constitutes 'harmful acts directed at an individual or group of individuals based on their gender' (UNCHR, 2021). GBV has been identified as one of the strongest sociocultural risk factors associated with the development of mental health problems in resettled refugee women and is a significant risk factor for PTSD in this population (Borrocks et al., 2022; Vallejo-Martin et al., 2021). Borrocks et al. (2022) surveyed 507 clinic-attending refugee women in Jordan …

Draws a conclusion	Evidence on the gendered realities and impact of traumatic experiences for refugee women in their pre-migration journeys suggests the need for more gender-specific screening procedures for PTSD. This is particularly important in light of emerging evidence on the complex layers of post-migration stressors they are likely to encounter as they continue their journeys in the host country.
Anticipates next theme	
Theme 2	**2.2 Exposure to post-migration stressors …**

Concluding your literature review

How you conclude your review depends on its purpose.

Critical reviews of the literature

Your reader might expect you to explain briefly:

- **What** did you aim to achieve, and **how**: A reminder about the question you set out to answer and the method you used.
- **So what** did you find? A summary of the conclusions you've reached in answer to your question and why you've reached those conclusions.
- **Now what?** A recommendation about the way forward in terms of research and practice related to your question – your recommendations based on what you found in the literature.

To conclude your review, you could do something like this:

Summary of what you've done
- aim/purpose of the review
- how you did it

→ The purpose of this critical review was to...
→ Qualitative and quantitative evidence on X dated between ... was critically analysed ...

Your evidence-based conclusions e.g.
- what is the most effective practice/approach?
- what are the gaps in knowledge on the topic & why is this a concern?

→ A large number of studies have examined X and they provide compelling evidence that ...
→ However, much of the research on the topic is quantitative, which means that there is very limited understanding about Y ...
→ This is concerning, given the varied experiences recorded in the small body of research exploring the topic. While limited in number, they suggest that current interventions might be ...

Implications of your findings for research & current practice/policy in topic area
- your recommendations based on findings
- acknowledgement of limitations of your review

→ The findings of this critical review of the literature suggest that policy and practice guidelines could benefit from a review in terms of ... While this review has focused on a relatively small number of studies in a limited time-period, the findings suggest a concerning ...

Drafting your literature review

Justifying a research topic

For a dissertation or thesis, you've critically analysed existing contributions to the conversation on the topic to make a space for your own research. Now is the time to make your intended new contribution to the conversation clear. This could be in terms of:

- testing a theory in a new context
- using a new or adapted approach to analysing your data
- collecting new data on the topic.

To conclude your review, you can do something like this:

Summary of state of knowledge on topic
– what is known/understood
– gaps/limitations in knowledge

→ Although prior research has established the physiological and demographic factors associated with X, there has been limited research on how patients experience the pain associated with this condition in different settings …

Reference to study(s) closest to yours and limitations in terms of your topic

→ One recent study examined …; however …

Specific gap that your research will address & indication of originality (if relevant)

Why it's important to address gap

How your study addresses gap

→ To the best of my knowledge, this is the first study that explores the personal pain experiences of patients with this condition in the Y setting. Insights into the personal experiences of patients in this setting are important because current pain management protocols are failing to address …

→ Therefore, this study set out to explore patient pain experiences during diagnostic procedures, treatment procedures …

Your intended contribution by filling gap

→ Giving a voice to patients can contribute to a deeper understanding of diverse psychosocial and physical needs, as well as coping mechanisms in this setting …

Drafting your literature review

Review of the literature using systematic methods

You've presented and interpreted the results of your analysis for the reader in your results and discussion sections. In the Conclusion, your reader wants to know:

- **What** did you conclude? Provide a definitive answer to your original question.
- **So what** does it mean? Give the reader a clear indication of what they can take away from your review.
- **What now**? Recommend what can be done with this knowledge.

You might have quite specific instructions on how to structure your Conclusion. This is one example of how you could organise it:

```
┌─────────────────────────────┐         While research on dance therapy with
│  Summarised answer to       │ ······· post-stroke patients shows considerable
│  question – what is your    │         promise, there is currently insufficient
│  key conclusion about the   │         evidence to support systematic
│  evidence on your topic?    │         incorporation of the intervention into
└──────────────┬──────────────┘         current care programmes.
               ▼
┌─────────────────────────────┐         This review has contributed to the growing
│  Contribution of your       │ ······· body of evidence on the use of … Specifically,
│  review to knowledge on     │         it provides a systematic review of the
│  topic                      │         qualitative and quantitative evidence on …
│                             │
│  Limitations of your        │         A significant number of the studies used
│  review & what they mean    │ ······· self-reported measures of …. This means that
│  in terms of what readers   │         social desirability bias could have affected
│  can take away from your    │         … Furthermore, the relatively small sample
│  findings                   │         sizes in the studies … These factors mean
└──────────────┬──────────────┘         that the results of the studies must be viewed
               ▼                        with caution … However, the consistently
                                        high acceptability ratings across the studies
                                        suggests that …
┌─────────────────────────────┐
│  Implications of your       │         For professionals with access to resources for
│  findings for research      │ ······· this therapy, the associated benefits suggest
│  and current practice/      │         continued incorporation …
│  policy – your              │
│  recommendations based      │         Further research with larger sample groups
│  on your findings           │         could provide …
└─────────────────────────────┘
```

Drafting your literature review

Writing your Introduction

You're only ready to write your Introduction once you've finished the rest of your review, including the conclusion. The Introduction tells the reader what to expect in terms of what you'll be covering, and you might make changes once you start writing your first draft. It does happen, despite the best planning!

The Introduction is your opportunity to convince the reader that your topic is worth investigating and to establish the boundaries of your investigation. A useful way to think about it is that you're taking the reader through a series of interconnected 'moves' leading the reader down to the aim of your review. This may be done in a single paragraph or two paragraphs, a section, or a whole chapter, depending on the requirements for your project.

Each move presents an argument on why your review is needed:

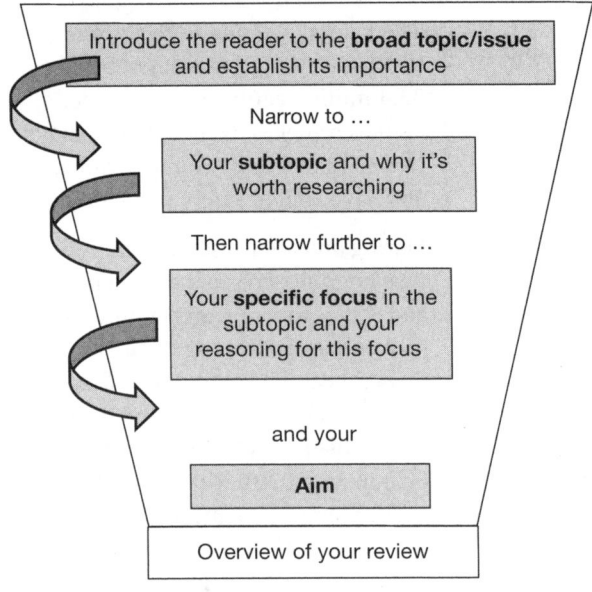

Introduces **broad topic/issue** and establishes importance with notable statistics	The United Nations High Commission for Refugees (UNHCR) (2023) estimates that there are currently 36.4 million **refugee**s worldwide. The UNHCR defines refugees as 'people who have fled their countries to escape conflict, violence or persecution and have sought safety in another country'.
Narrows to **subtopic** and explains why it's an area worth researching	During and after resettlement, refugees often face ongoing stressors related to legal processes and socioeconomic and cultural issues in their host countries, leaving them highly vulnerable to mental health disorders such as anxiety, depression, prolonged grief disorder and **post-traumatic stress disorder (PTSD)** (Bryant et al., 2020, 2023; Freedman, 2020). Although refugees undergo an immigration medical examination (IME) to determine their health status on arrival in their host countries, the screening is often limited to physical health, and mental health problems such as PTSD often remain undiagnosed (Magwood et al., 2023).

	This can have a detrimental effect on wellbeing after resettlement. …
Narrows to **specific focus in subtopic** and provides **reasoning** for this focus	**Resettled women refugees** face unique vulnerabilities related to the nature of their experiences, which makes them particularly vulnerable to PTSD beyond initial resettlement (Dekinger et al., 2021; Mundy et al., 2020). …
	However, current policy and practice guidelines often do not reflect the complex vulnerabilities of resettled women refugees (Vasquez Corona et al., 2024).
	Thus, service providers in host countries can miss opportunities to identify women at risk for the condition and recommend appropriate actions. …
Presents aim of critical review	**The purpose** of this critical review is to analyse current evidence on the risk factors and most effective interventions for PTSD in resettled women refugees.

11 Editing your literature review

You'll be drafting and redrafting throughout the writing process. When you're feeling confident that you have a finished draft, stand back, give yourself a break and then look at it with fresh eyes.

Checking the big picture

Have you answered the question you set out to answer?

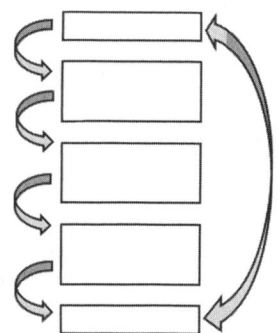

- Does your Introduction establish the boundaries of your topic?
- Do each of your sections develop arguments within the boundaries of this topic?
- Are your arguments in sections and/or paragraphs organised in a logical order?
- Is your Conclusion justified by your arguments?
- Is there a clear link between your Introduction and your Conclusion?

DOING YOUR LITERATURE REVIEW

Checking your arguments

Will your reader be convinced by each of your arguments?

- Is your reasoning clear? Have you signposted your argument for the reader?
- Have you provided enough evidence to persuade the reader that your perceptions of the literature are sound?
- Is your use of information accurate? For example, are authors' ideas and findings presented as intended?

Have you defined terminology and abstract concepts or ideas for the reader?

Polishing your draft

Here, you'll be looking for spelling, punctuation, style and grammar issues, errors that are often overlooked when you're tired. For example, have you avoided overly long sentences and jargon?

You may want to read your draft aloud or hear it being read aloud. This can help you decide whether what you've written make sense. It's easy to read over mistakes or issues in your text. Use tools, such as Read Aloud (available in MS Word), or any apps that read text aloud for you.

If you plan to make use of AI tools to assist the proofreading and editing process, first check your university guidance so that you are clear about what is and is not permitted. No piece of writing is perfect; there are multiple – equally valid – ways in which to approach an assignment. If you ask AI tools for suggestions about how to improve your writing, you will always be given suggestions: don't let this undermine your confidence in what you have produced.

Throughout this guide, we've shown you examples of how gen AI tools can be used to assist you: from formulating questions and generating ideas to refining your writing. You are not using these tools to do the writing itself. Remember, you are the conductor of the review: you select the voices in the academic conversation you decide to join, you bring them together, and critically evaluate what they bring to the conversation, so you can share your new insights on the topic of review.

A final word

Some of you might have reached your final destination with the Conclusion of your literature review.

For others, the literature review has provided a solid foundation for your research or a related project and signals the start of a new phase in your journey.

Thank you for travelling with us to where you are. We hope you've found our advice helpful!

References

Burke, K. (1941) *The philosophy of literary form*. University of California Press.

Coonan, E. (2020) *Where's your evidence?* Bloomsbury.

Dang, D., Dearholt, S. L. Bissett, K., Ascenzi, J., and Whalen, M. (2021) *John Hopkins evidence-based practice for nurses and healthcare professionals: Models and guidelines* (4th edn). Sigma Theta Tau International.

Godfrey, J. (2023) *Reading and making notes* (3rd edn). Bloomsbury.

Jones, A. (2007) Ask the professor about … good literature reviews. *MAI Review, 1*. www.journal.mai.ac.nz/system/files/maireview/43-43-1-PB.pdf

Lenton, A. (2016) Retired athletes: When the spotlight dims, MA thesis. Massey University, Albany.

Melnyk, B. and Fineout-Overholt, E. (2023) *Evidence-based practice in nursing & healthcare: A guide to best practice* (5th edn). Wolters Kluwer.

Morley, J. (2023) *Academic phrasebank*. Manchester University. www.phrasebank.manchester.ac.uk

The Open University (2025) *Critically processing what you read.* https://help.open.ac.uk/critical-reading-techniques/critically-processing-what-you-read

World Health Organization (2018) *New series published to support the use of qualitative research in decision-making.* www.who.int/news/item/18-01-2018-new-series-published-to-support-the-use-of-qualitative-research-in-decision-making

Williams, K. (2022) *Getting critical* (3rd edn). Bloomsbury.

Williams, K. and Reid, M. (2023) *Planning your dissertation* (3rd edn). Bloomsbury.

Index

annotated bibliography 66–8
argument vii-viii, 63, 74, 88–93, 101–4, 106–8

CASP 58
conclusion 7, 9, 12, 114–19
contribution
    of sources ix–xi, 8, 12, 54–6, 64–7, 98
    your own 116–17, 119
critical
    analysis 5, 84, 115–16
    discussion of research 98–104
    evaluation 6, 8
    reviews 8–10, 14, 81, 114–15
    voice 105–8

databases xi, 11–13, 39–46, 61
    searching 42–6

editing 124–6
eligibility criteria 11, 41, 61
evaluation 6–8, 57–9, 63, 107–11
    criteria 47–50
evidence viii, 2–12, 38, 49, 53, 105–6
    evaluating 10, 12, 58, 109–11
    levels of 17–20
    synthesising 88–96

flow 96–8
formulating questions 31–2
framework 7, 32, 83–4, 99

gap xi, 6, 54, 60, 65, 115
    for own research 3, 6–7, 69, 103–4, 117
    highlighting 100–4
gen AI
    checkpoints for use xiv, 20–1, 126
    prompts 14–15, 33, 44, 70
    tools 44–5, 126
grey literature 37–9

inclusion/exclusion 58–60
    criteria 11–12, 41, 47–51, 61
introduction 5, 7, 9, 11–12, 54, 84, 110
    writing your 120–3

journal articles xi, 13, 23, 49–50, 69
    finding information 52–4
    peer reviewed 19, 27, 37, 49
    randomized controlled trials 18–20, 110
    systematic reviews 13, 17–18, 20, 38, 58, 61

key words 23, 41–7

limitations 8–9, 52, 54, 98, 100–7, 115–17
literature reviews
  as part of a larger project 3–7, 60–8, 116–17
  stand-alone 8–10, 14, 81, 114–15
  requiring systematic methods 10–13, 46, 58–61, 69, 118–19

method 10–11, 38, 61, 114, 118
methodology, 11–13, 46, 49, 53, 68–9, 85

notes 65–71

paragraph 2, 5, 91–3, 97–8, 120, 124
PICO(T) 31–2
planning 73–86
PRISMA 46, 61
prompts 14–15, 33, 44, 70

qualitative 17–20, 67, 101–2
quantitative 17–20, 110–11

randomized controlled trials 18–20, 110
rationale 103–4
reading 62–71
  grid 68
references
  grouping 93–6
  managing 57, 72, 79
research
  articles 13, 49, 52–4
  databases 40–6, 61
  question 24–6, 38, 83, 87, 109, 114
  primary/secondary 19

search strategy 26, 36–41, 46
  recording your 46
similarity/difference
  in findings 67, 79, 88, 93–6
sources
  types of 37–8
  evaluating 47–51

peer-reviewed 19, 28, 37, 40, 49
  primary/secondary 16
strategic questions 28–31
strengths 8–9, 54, 84, 98
structure 2–14, 80–6, 91–2, 112–14, 118
synthesis xi, 6–8, 63, 73–4, 88–96
  matrix 78–9

themes ix, 2, 9, 74–82
  identifying 76–9
  outlining 80–4
  structuring 112–14
theory xi, 7, 29, 31, 67, 99
  theoretical perspective 59, 83–4, 99
topic
  choosing 22–4
  focusing 25–34
  scope 2, 26, 33, 42, 55

voice 87, 105–8

Index 131